THE BARBARIAN KINGS

TREASURES OF THE WORLD

THE BARBARIAN KINGS

by
Lionel Casson

STONEHENGE

Treasures of the World was created by
Tree Communications, Inc.
and published by Stonehenge Press Inc.

TREE COMMUNICATIONS, INC.

PRESIDENT
Rodney Friedman

PUBLISHER
Bruce Michel

VICE PRESIDENTS
Ronald Gross
Paul Levin

EDITOR
Charles L. Mee, Jr.

EXECUTIVE EDITOR
Shirley Tomkievicz

ART DIRECTOR
Sara Burris

PICTURE EDITOR
Mary Zuazua Jenkins

ASSOCIATE EDITORS
Thomas Dickey   Vance Muse   Henry Wiencek

ASSISTANT ART DIRECTOR
Carole Muller

ASSISTANT PICTURE EDITORS
Deborah Bull   Carol Gaskin
Charlie Holland   Linda Silvestri Sykes

COPY EDITOR
Fredrica A. Harvey

ASSISTANT COPY EDITOR
Todd C. Martin

PRODUCTION ASSISTANTS
Eric Goldin   Peter Sparber

EDITORIAL ASSISTANTS
Martha J. Brown   Carol Epstein
Holly McLennon Wheelwright

FOREIGN RESEARCHERS
Rosemary Burgis (London) Sandra Diaz (Mexico City)
Eiko Fukuda (Tokyo) Bianca Spantigati Gabbrielli (Rome)
Mirka Gondicas (Athens) Patricia Hanna (Madrid)
Alice Jugie (Paris) Traudl Lessing (Vienna)
Dee Pattee (Munich) Brigitte Rückriegel (Bonn)
Simonetta Toraldo (Rome)

CONSULTING EDITORS
Joseph J. Thorndike, Jr.
Dr. Ulrich Hiesinger

STONEHENGE PRESS INC.

PUBLISHER
John Canova

EDITOR
Ezra Bowen

DEPUTY EDITOR
Carolyn Tasker

THE AUTHOR: Lionel Casson is the author of two other TREASURES volumes, *The Greek Conquerors* and *The Pharaohs*, as well as other works about life in ancient times. He is Andrew W. Mellon Professor of Classical Studies at the American Academy in Rome and professor of classics at New York University.

CONSULTANT FOR THIS BOOK: Katharine R. Brown, who wrote the *Guide to Provincial Roman and Barbarian Metalwork and Jewelry in the Metropolitan Museum of Art*, is senior research associate in the department of Medieval Art at the museum and helped organize the recent exhibition of Irish art treasures.

COVER: *Shining with gold, glass, and garnets, this ornament comes from the grave of an Anglo-Saxon king of about A.D. 600. At center is a man with two beasts rampant: possibly wild boars, sacred animals in early England.*

TITLE PAGE: *The Sigurd Helmet, of bronze, iron, and chain mail, takes its name from the dragon-slaying hero of Viking legends. In fact it belonged to a seventh-century Swedish chieftain.*

OVERLEAF: *In a detail from a masterfully wrought electrum urn of the fourth century B.C., a Scythian nomad, trousered to ride, trains his horse to kneel.*

ABOVE: *Before A.D. 600, Gothic tribesmen had settled in Spain, where they created such treasures as this gold and garnet clasp shaped like an eagle—a favored Gothic motif.*

CONTENTS

to Iceland c.900,
Greenland c.980, and
Newfoundland c.1000

FAROE
ISLANDS

SHETLAND
ISLANDS

c.840

c.780

787

NORTH
SEA

Oseberg ▲ • Oslo

Gokstad ▲

Birka ▲

BALTIC
SEA

ARRAN

LINDISFARNE

c.450

c.450

c.850

GOTLAND

Gundestrup ▲

JUTLAND

SKELLIGS

c.400 B.C.

c.400 B.C.

c.450

c.850

Hedeby ▲

c.250

c.150

Sutton
Hoo ▲

London
Thames

c.450

c.815

Boulogne

446

Cologne

c.400

Ebro

Oder

ATLANTIC
OCEAN

Bayeux

Tournai

Soissons

Reims

Paris
Seine

c.600 B.C.

Vix

Rhine

Tours
Loire

c.450

Alesia

Danube

c.400 B.C.

c.430

Poitiers

c.490

Lyon

410

Garonne

Rhône

c.390 B.C.

ALPS

Milan

Pavia

Po

Mantua

c.450

c.370

c.450 B.C.

PYRENEES

Toulouse

c.420

Elbe

Marseille

c.415

Ravenna

489

409

Pisa

c.400

Lisbon

c.420

Toledo

Barcelona

Rome

c.280 B.C.

Seville

Cadiz

c.845

STRAIT OF
GIBRALTAR

c.455

c.410

Delph

c.435

Carthage ▲

MEDITERRANEAN
SEA

0   400 Miles

0   400 Kilometers

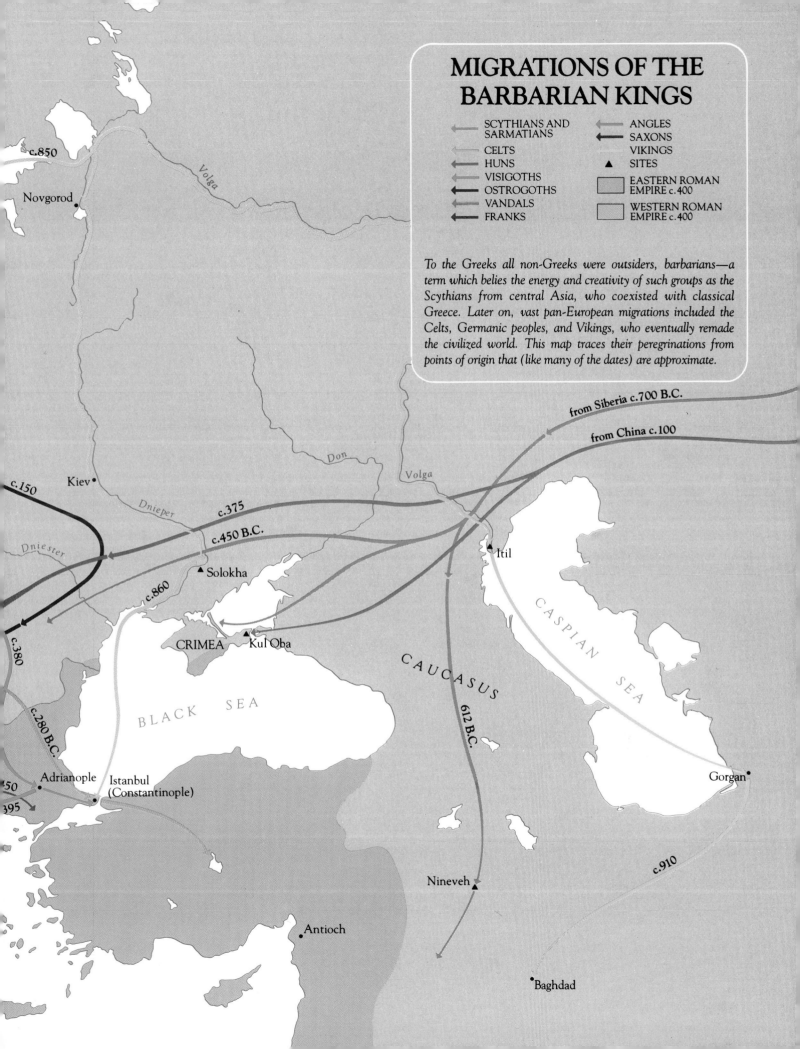

MIGRATIONS OF THE BARBARIAN KINGS

SCYTHIANS AND SARMATIANS
CELTS
HUNS
VISIGOTHS
OSTROGOTHS
VANDALS
FRANKS

ANGLES
SAXONS
VIKINGS
▲ **SITES**
EASTERN ROMAN EMPIRE c. 400
WESTERN ROMAN EMPIRE c. 400

To the Greeks all non-Greeks were outsiders, barbarians—a term which belies the energy and creativity of such groups as the Scythians from central Asia, who coexisted with classical Greece. Later on, vast pan-European migrations included the Celts, Germanic peoples, and Vikings, who eventually remade the civilized world. This map traces their peregrinations from points of origin that (like many of the dates) are approximate.

c.850

Novgorod

Volga

from Siberia c.700 B.C.

from China c.100

Don

Volga

c.150

Kiev

Dnieper

c.375

c.450 B.C.

Itil

Dniester

c.860

Solokha

CASPIAN SEA

c.380

CRIMEA

Kul Oba

c.280 B.C.

CAUCASUS

Adrianople

Istanbul (Constantinople)

450

395

BLACK SEA

612 B.C.

Gorgan

c.910

Nineveh

Antioch

c.850

Baghdad

I

OUTSIDE THE PALE

AMONG THE SCYTHIANS

A Scythian, after killing his first man, drinks his blood. He cuts off the heads of all he kills in battle and brings them to the king. Whoever brings a head shares in whatever booty they take; no head, no share. He flays a head as follows: making a circular cut above the ears, he grasps it and shakes loose the scalp. Then he scrapes off the flesh with the bone of an ox, kneads the scalp with his hands, and, having softened it, has got himself a sort of handkerchief. He ties it to the bridle of his riding horse and shows it off. Whoever has the most such handkerchiefs is considered the champion. Many Scythians make cloaks to wear out of the scalps, sewing them together like sheepskin coats. Many flay the right hands of the enemy dead, fingernails and all, to make quiver-covers. . . .

So reported Herodotus, the inquisitive and sharp-eyed Greek travel-writer and historian, who about 450 B.C. paid a visit to south Russia, the homeland of the Scythians, traveling by ship along the coast of the Black Sea. His account is the very first glimpse on record into the lives of the multitudinous peoples who lived beyond the pale of ancient civilization. Without Herodotus and later Greek and

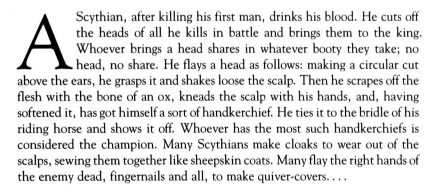

Scythian archers draw their bows on a fourth-century-B.C. plaque. Great fighters, the Scythians dominated the south Russian steppe for over half a millennium.

A spear-wielding Scythian charges forth on his mount. These nomads rode without stirrups, sitting forward in the saddle and clamping the horse with knees and calves. The animals' relatively small size also helped make them manageable.

Roman travelers who took an interest in exotic manners and morals on the fringes of the classical world, the barbarians would be a greater mystery than they are. Some of them—most spectacularly the Scythians—left extravagant works of art buried in their graves. From these treasures, as well as from the Greek and Latin accounts—by marveling but often condescending visitors—comes all that history can tell about these remarkable tribes.

The word "barbarian" derives from the Greek *barbaros*, which originally meant merely "foreign"; the Greeks applied it to any person whose language they could not understand, whose language was gibberish to them and sounded like a reiterated "bar-bar-bar." The essential characteristic of such people was that they were outsiders; they not only were outside the pale of Greek and Roman habitation but outside the Greek and Roman conception of how people should live. But later the word took on negative connotations: *barbaroi* were people who had never been softened by the effects of civilization, of city living; people who, often having no settled home, were rude and simple in their ways and, above all, presumably lacked that measure of respect for fellow human beings that civilization is meant to inculcate. The soldier of a civilized nation, having killed an enemy in battle, strips him of everything of value; the barbarian warrior did that too but, according to Greek accounts of them, also made a handkerchief out of his scalp.

Another mark of the barbarian is the simplified social and political organization he lives under. The Greeks and Romans, for example, knew the full range of political forms: monarchy, republic, democracy. Moreover, their political units had a recognized geography marked by well-defined frontiers. The peoples who lived beyond the rim of Greco-Roman civilization were organized in tribes headed by chieftains, and these tribes often wandered at will with no fixed periphery or, if they did limit their movements to a given area, rarely established formal boundaries.

The leader of a group of tribes, or of a notably powerful tribe, might bear the title of king and enjoy royal honors. Among the Scythians the greatest of these honors came at death. When one of their rulers passed away, they dug a big square pit and set his body in it upon a mattress. Then, reported Herodotus,

> they strangle and bury in the open space left about the body one of his concubines, his cupbearer, cook, groom, valet, messenger, and his horses, along with the first pick of all else he owned and his gold cups (Scythians do not use silver or bronze cups). . . . After a year has passed. . . they take fifty of the most suitable of the rest of his servants and strangle them along with fifty of the finest horses. They gut the bodies, stuff them with chaff, and sew them up. . . . They run a thick stake through the horses from tail to neck and plant them [on special stands so that]. . . their legs dangle in air. . . . They mount each of the fifty strangled youths on a horse. . . by driving through the corpses along the spine up to the neck a straight pole, leaving a part projecting below which they set into a socket in the stake through the horse. These horsemen they arrange in a circle around the tomb.

Fortunately there were more appealing items included in a royal burial. Herodotus mentions gold cups and other assorted riches. And as excavation of dozens of Scythians tombs has revealed, barbarian kings took a range of treasure to their graves. The deceased were laid away dressed in their most elegant clothes and surrounded by their most prized possessions. In the fourth century B.C. at Solokha, along the Dnieper River north of the Crimea, Scythians buried the body of a king decked with a gold torque about his neck and five gold bracelets on his arms—three on the right and two on the left—and covered by a pall on which were sewn no less than three hundred gold plaques. They placed a wooden cup set in gold nearby, a sword with a gold handle, a magnificent gold comb, and seven silver vases.

Herodotus visited the land of the Scythians during their heyday, when they had settled down after centuries of wandering. They were a Persian-speaking people who originally were from somewhere in Siberia northeast of Persia, but left this region to migrate south and west. A main branch went more or less directly to south Russia and about 700 B.C. came to rest there. A smaller branch was more adventurous. They made their way through Persia into the Near East fighting, conquering, looting, and causing no end of trouble. First

In this detail from a fourth-century-B.C. vase, a long-haired Scythian warrior clasps a shield and spear. The costume he wears—close-fitting belted tunic and trousers tucked into high boots—was good for both riding and protection in harsh weather.

they joined forces with the Assyrians, the lords of the area, whose capital city was Nineveh. Together these ferocious allies conquered the Medes, who lived south of the Caspian Sea. At one point the Scythians raided their way through Palestine as far south as the borders of Egypt and prepared to wreak havoc on this rich prize, but the pharaoh managed to buy them off.

Next they turned around and joined the Medes and the Babylonians, who now were struggling to break Assyrian power. In 612 B.C. this triple alliance besieged, plundered, and razed the great city of Nineveh. But the Medes eventually had enough of these volatile allies. Herodotus says that the king of the Medes invited them to a banquet, got them roaring drunk, and then massacred every one of them. The facts were less picturesque: the Medes harried them until they exited from Persia, at which point they elected to turn westward and join their brethren in south Russia.

The Scythians settled down in south Russia only in the sense that they no longer indulged in far-flung wanderings. They turned the indigenous farming folk into vassals and forced them to supply grain and other necessities. They themselves, congenital nomads, were forever on the move—the men on horseback and their families in ox-drawn wagons that were veritable mobile homes, divided into two or three cubicles and roofed with a felt cover. Though the Scythians kept herds of cattle, the horse was the linchpin of their existence: it carried the men into battle and the hunt, it supplied some of their basic food—cheese and dried curd made from mare's milk— and it furnished the national drink, *kumys*, which was fermented mare's milk.

Life among the Scythians focused on the male—women were totally subordinate—and warfare provided life's greatest moments: victory in battle brought recognition and rewards to the survivors, honorable burial to the slain, and a joyous celebration for everybody. The Scythian warriors were mounted archers whose forte was rushing at an enemy, discharging a volley of arrows, and then dashing back to safety. The horses they rode upon were small but tough and fast Asiatic ponies, and the bows they held were short—

An elegant steppe horseman, who carries a gorytus —a bow-and-arrow case—at his waist, approaches a severe-looking woman, who is probably a goddess. Seated on a throne, she holds a stylized tree. The figures adorn a tapestry from the tomb of a fourth-century-B.C. noble in Siberia.

about two and a half feet in length—and hence had only a limited range; but they shot an arrow with tremendous velocity.

Only through battle did a Scythian achieve manhood—by killing an enemy and wearing the badge of a scalp to prove it, as Herodotus describes. The seasoned veteran added drinking cups carved from the skulls of especially worthy opponents. Since a Scythian spent a large part of the time on horseback, he dressed in suitable garb: a close-fitting sleeved tunic belted about the waist, boots of soft leather, and tight trousers. The last item of apparel aroused much comment among the Greeks since they never wore them, preferring tunics or robes. A trousered Scythian striding down the street created a great stir in a Greek town. South Russia gets cold during the winter, so the Scythians had appropriate garments—leather jackets, often trimmed with fur, and peaked hoods.

The clothing the Scythians wore, or at least those who could afford it, was gorgeously decorated with embroidery and appliqué. On great occasions they decked themselves with a full complement of glittering gold jewelry: headbands, pendants, earrings (in one ear for men, in both for women), bracelets, finger rings. At these times they invariably feasted, and the tableware was as gorgeous as the people: gold cups, ivory-handled knives, gold and silver jugs. In one particularly rich tomb the Scythians buried a two-foot-high jug for kumys. Made of electrum, a natural alloy of silver and gold, it is decorated with the Scythian equivalent of a cowboy scene: a pair of young men with lassos are rounding up a bunch of grazing ponies.

Although kumys was the drink of choice, contact with the Greeks living nearby generated a taste for wine, especially among the nobles. Indeed, drinking from a mighty bowlful of wine was the major event at an annual get-together in honor of all warriors who had a scalp to their credit. Those who had not yet achieved this distinction had to stay off to the side, ashamed and disregarded; those who had a great number to their credit were allowed to help themselves to two cupfuls at a time. The food at these celebrations was usually horsemeat or mutton stewed in a huge copper caldron.

The longest parties were those that preceded a funeral—forty

TEXT CONTINUED ON PAGE 20

THE WELL-CLAD HORSE

The Scythians owed much of their prowess to horses. If not the first riders in history, they were probably the earliest to tame the wild steppe pony and to master the art of horsemanship. Indeed the Scythians' culture spread to tribes scattered across the Eurasian steppes—all of them natural and gifted horsemen. Aggressive and free, they naturally felt superior to men on foot, who in turn regarded them with a mixture of fear and awe.

The steppe riders outfitted their horses as handsomely as themselves, with trappings that included colorful saddles, harnesses festooned with beautifully carved wooden plaques, and elaborate masks. This finery, faultlessly crafted and typically decorated with vigorous animal forms, also went to the grave; for when a chieftain died, the tribe slaughtered his best horses and buried them, fully caparisoned, in his tomb. Since they were made of highly perishable materials, few such ornaments from the Black Sea region have survived. However, the pieces here and on the next two pages belonged to rich warlords akin to the Scythians who lived some 2,500 miles to the east, high in the Altai Mountains of Siberia. There, layers of permafrost fortuitously preserved the horse gear they took to their graves 2,400 years ago—fabulous treasures that embody the very essence of the mounted nomad's way of life.

On the seat of the leather-and-felt saddle cover opposite, an appliquéd griffin seizes a mountain goat; the pendants, bordered with horsehair and fur, bear a motif of horned animals. A rider spread this cover over his saddle—two pillows stuffed with reindeer hair.

Made of leather trimmed with fur and gold foil, the mask above completely covered a horse's head. The ornament has perforated ear sheaths and a crest portraying mythical beasts battling one another.

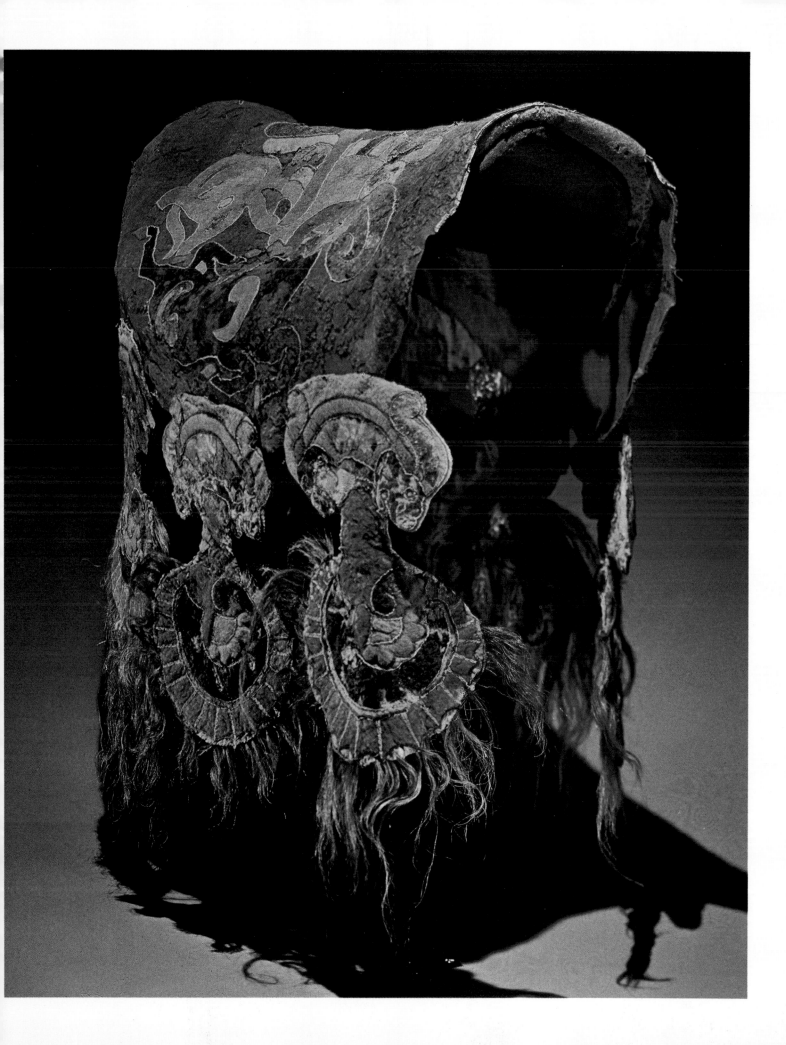

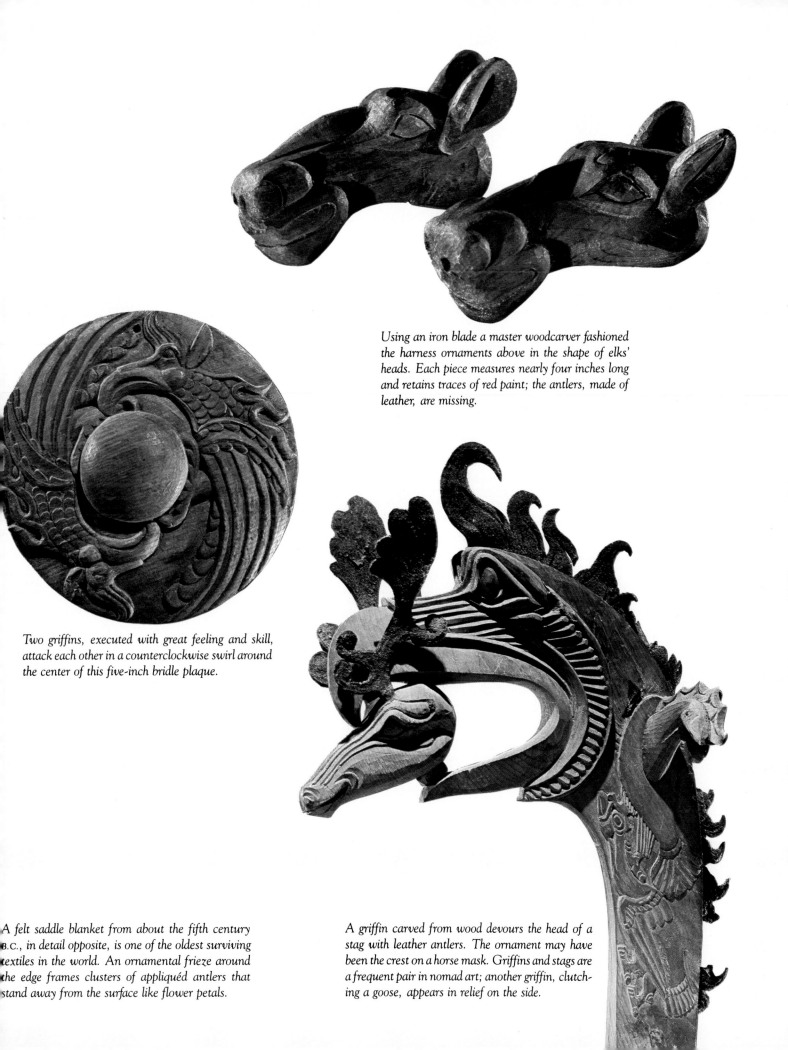

Using an iron blade a master woodcarver fashioned the harness ornaments above in the shape of elks' heads. Each piece measures nearly four inches long and retains traces of red paint; the antlers, made of leather, are missing.

Two griffins, executed with great feeling and skill, attack each other in a counterclockwise swirl around the center of this five-inch bridle plaque.

A felt saddle blanket from about the fifth century B.C., in detail opposite, is one of the oldest surviving textiles in the world. An ornamental frieze around the edge frames clusters of appliquéd antlers that stand away from the surface like flower petals.

A griffin carved from wood devours the head of a stag with leather antlers. The ornament may have been the crest on a horse mask. Griffins and stags are a frequent pair in nomad art; another griffin, clutching a goose, appears in relief on the side.

A woman wearing a short skirt dances with her arms held high and hands clasped. This gold plaque is from the grave of a Scythian priestess who served the Greek fertility goddess Demeter and may have danced at festivals for the deity.

TEXT CONTINUED FROM PAGE 15

days of continuous banqueting, according to Herodotus. After the funeral all who attended cleansed themselves of the association with death in two ways: their heads by a thorough washing and their bodies by what Herodotus calls a "hot-airing." They built a tepee-like tent, put in a brazier full of hot coals, crawled in clutching a handful of hemp, placed it on the stones, sniffed the fumes, and, to quote his words, "get such pleasure from this 'hot-airing' that they howl out loud." Apparently the hemp was pure hashish.

Death and its rites were a key aspect of the Scythians' religion. They worshiped various deities, the chief of whom was the goddess Tabiti, often pictured presiding over the administering of oaths or the anointing of chieftains. Sometimes she is a winged female surrounded by her sacred beasts, a raven and a dog. The stag was also a sacred animal, perhaps a totem or symbol of the tribe. None of the deities had temples or shrines, and the Scythians raised altars to only one god, the god of war. They would forgather at a given place to worship, carry on their devotions, and then abandon it, selecting some other spot for the next convocation.

Nor were there priests among them. The only formal clerical body that they had was an order of prophets, who were regularly called in by the king to deliver forecasts or to explain the obscure in matters of great moment. One such moment was when the king himself fell ill. The standard procedure then was for him to summon the three top prophets to reveal the cause, and their standard reply (at least according to Herodotus) was that a certain person had "sworn falsely by the royal hearth," the most solemn oath a Scythian could take. Naturally the accused would deny the charge. The mechanism for appeal was to summon half a dozen additional prophets. If they upheld the judgment of the original trio, the accused was forthwith beheaded; if first they and then still more prophets called in on the case upheld the man's innocence, the initial trio were forthwith burned alive. Prophecy could be a dangerous business.

The Scythians kept to their own way of life even though, as time went on, they had increasing commerce with other peoples, especially the Greeks, who from about 650 B.C. on planted colonies all about the Black Sea. The Scythians maintained a brisk trade with these, exchanging cattle and furs and grain for wine and the products of Greek craftsmanship. This is plainly visible in the decoration of the Scythian jewelry, armor, horse trappings, vases, cups, and other objects that come from Scythian tombs. The earlier pieces, made in the seventh and sixth centuries B.C., reflect for the most part Scythian taste, especially the predilection for stylized figures of animals; the stag, a prized symbol, was a particular favorite. Starting about the fifth century B.C., the objects show increasing Greek influence. The scenes may be of Scythian life—a Scythian stringing a bow or in combat or helping a wounded comrade—but the treatment is typically Greek. Or the scenes themselves as well as the treatment may be typically Greek—a head of Athena or a battle between Greeks and Persians. The best are clearly the work of Greek craftsmen; the less expert could have been made by Scythian craftsmen trained under Greek masters.

Though Scythians and Greeks were in close contact, though the twain met and frequently, they lived their lives apart. The Greeks developed an ever more sophisticated urban existence, while the Scythians stuck stubbornly to their nomadic groups or primitive villages. Herodotus tells a story that well illustrates the point. A certain Scythian king, Scylas, happened to be half Greek; his father had married a woman from a Greek colony on the coast of what is today Rumania. Their son had an irresistible craving for things Greek. In the course of time he managed to work out a solution: he set up a secret household complete with wife in the closest Greek town, and he would sneak off from his graceless village to spend a delicious month or more living *à la grecque.* He went so far as to get gloriously drunk with the Greek mobs celebrating the festival of the wine god Dionysus. This was too much. Some eyewitness blabbed to his subjects, and they hunted him down and beheaded him.

Cheek to cheek, two Scythians take an oath by sharing the same drinking horn, a ritual that the Greek historian Herodotus described. The participants would mingle drops of their blood with wine and dip weapons into the mixture before drinking it.

A bearded, wide-shouldered warrior carved in stone holds an ox-horn cup in his right hand and a sword in his left. This figure was the grave monument at a royal Scythian tomb in the southern Ukraine, the region where the Scythians last held sway.

The Scythians held the niche they had carved out in history for well over half a millennium, as late as the second century A.D. Then they succumbed to their eastern neighbors, a people called the Sarmatians. These had always shared the Scythians' nomadic mode of life. They, too, lived on horseback, carried their families in felt-covered wagons, and subsisted on game, horsemeat, and mare's milk. They wore the long trousers and soft leather boots of steppe nomads, and according to Strabo, the Greek geographer who observed their habits in the first century A.D., the Sarmatians had nothing but contempt for those who went on foot. Like Scythians they made war on horseback but with one signal advantage over their adversaries: Sarmatian women fought alongside the men, and fought savagely. Their distant ancestors may have been the inspiration for the Amazons of Greek mythology. But in the course of time, as they moved westward off the steppe, the Sarmatians gained yet another advantage: they gave up the small, fast pony and use of bows and arrows. Instead they covered both themselves and their mounts with a carapace of heavy armor and wielded either long lances or swords so big they had to be gripped with both hands. The Sarmatians, in fact, were the precursors of the medieval European knight. The Scythians, unable to resist this formidable cavalry, were reduced to vassals and eventually disappeared from history. By the fourth century A.D., the Sarmatians themselves had migrated into eastern Europe and vanished as a distinct people.

The fashioners, wearers, and users of treasure disappear. Yet if circumstances are kindly, the treasure itself can live on to delight the eye and stir the admiration of endless generations. The Scythians who decked themselves with glittering jewelry and drank out of cups of precious metals, and the craftsmen who made these objects for them, have long since ceased to be. But because their religious beliefs dictated that they were to go to their eternal rest dressed in all the finery they wore when alive and surrounded by the riches they enjoyed when they were alive, their treasures have triumphantly survived—treasures, what is more, of rare beauty and absolute uniqueness.

MASTERPIECES
ON THE MOVE

On a nomad's belt buckle of gold and turquoise, a frenzied
battle takes place: an eagle assaults a yak (at left), as a
feline (lower right) bites the eagle's tail.

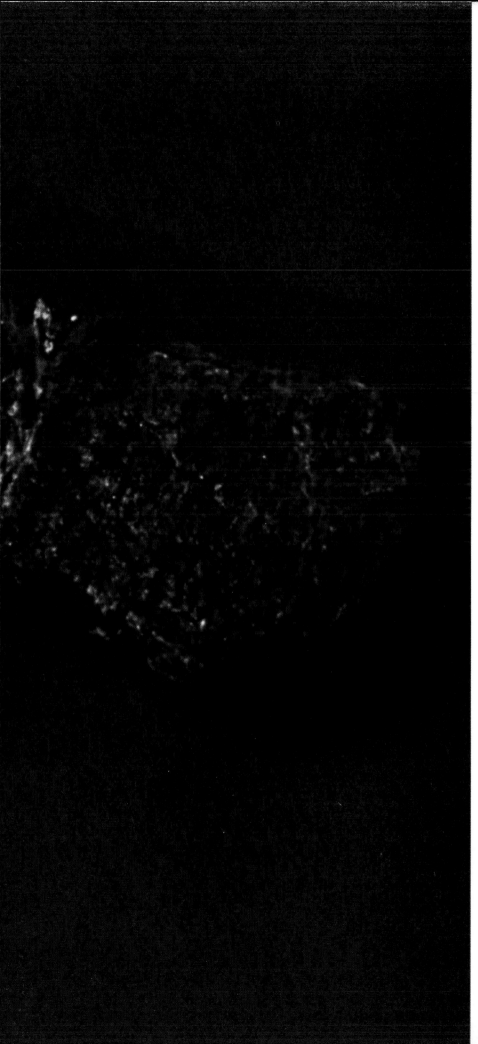

The Scythians of the Russian steppe, unlike
their sedentary Greek neighbors to the
south, had a passion almost solely for objects
that they could carry with them in their treks
across the grasslands. These warrior-herdsmen
particularly loved jewelry, flashy ornaments for
clothing and weapons, and a variety of splendid
vessels. For the kings among them, virtually all
these objects were fashioned from gold, which
the Scythians imported from mines in the Caucasus and other mountain ranges.

During the fifth and fourth centuries B.C.,
when Scythian culture was at its zenith, the
nomads matched their lavish use of gold with a
fondness for the work of Greek artisans living in
colonies on the north shore of the Black Sea.
Many of the pieces in this portfolio, recovered
from royal Scythian graves, were made by Greek
hands; yet they thoroughly reflect Scythian
taste, being embellished with scenes of nomads
or with powerful portrayals of the animals so
much a part of life on the steppe. The meaning
of the felines, stags, horses, and other beasts,
usually shown in taut poses, is elusive—in some
instances they were probably magical, intended
to ward off evil or impart strength to the owner.
But whether religious or purely decorative, this
bold, exuberant art style—which centuries later
figured in the trappings of other nomadic tribes
penetrating into Europe—amply satisfied the
Scythians' need for beauty and stood as permanent glittering tokens of their power.

Embossed gold encases the iron blade and handle of
a magnificent ceremonial ax—here in detail—en-
tombed with a Scythian lord in the sixth century B.C.
The ornamental display of panthers, stags, goats,
and other animals in various poses combines beasts
commonly known to the Scythians with more exotic
animals: the upright rams on the ax head are a
favorite motif of the ancient Persians.

25

26

A favorite Scythian subject—warriors in full pan-
oply—appears on one side of a fourth-century-B.C.
drinking cup, here nearly twice its actual size, from a
royal burial northeast of the Black Sea. Beautifully
worked by Greek craftsmen, the hands and faces are
modeled in silver; the hair, garments, and weapons
in gold. Each man holds a bow; the one on the right
also grips a sword, while his friend rests an arm on
his bow-and-arrow case.

OVERLEAF: Part of a burial treasure containing a
Scythian noble's battle gear, this great golden fish—a
sixteen-inch-long plaque made in the fifth century
B.C.—teems with a menagerie of other beasts. Rams'
heads jut from its tail, and raised across its body are
an eagle, a school of fish, a deer, and wildcats
fighting a boar.

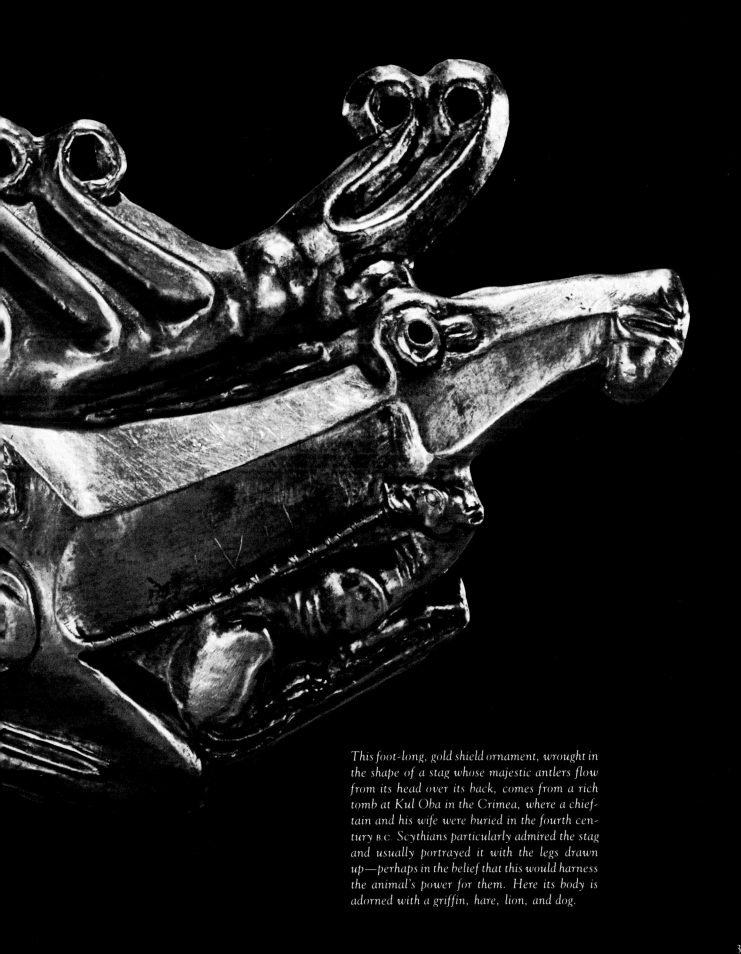

This foot-long, gold shield ornament, wrought in the shape of a stag whose majestic antlers flow from its head over its back, comes from a rich tomb at Kul Oba in the Crimea, where a chieftain and his wife were buried in the fourth century B.C. Scythians particularly admired the stag and usually portrayed it with the legs drawn up—perhaps in the belief that this would harness the animal's power for them. Here its body is adorned with a griffin, hare, lion, and dog.

ARMED SCYTHIANS CONVERSING

STRINGING A BOW

From the royal tomb at Kul Oba comes this gleaming gold vase, in four views, that lay at the feet of the king's consort. Almost actual size, it bears vignettes in relief of Scythians engaged in comradely activities, possibly after a battle. All of them wear tunics, boots, and trousers stitched with what seem to be decorative plaques.

DRESSING A LEG WOUND

TREATING A TOOTHACHE

Two hirsute horsemen, each of them only one and a half inches high, straddle the ends of a gold torque, or collar, that encircled the neck of the Scythian ruler buried at Kul Oba. The splendid figures are joined to the torque, which is made of plaited gold strands, by gold sheaths inlaid with bright blue and green enamel.

In a tableau of gold, a warrior reclines under a tree with his head on a woman's lap; above him hangs his quiver, and nearby are two horses and another man, perhaps a groom. This six-inch plaque from a Siberian grave was worn on a belt or sword. The image of the cavalier sleeping on his lady's lap probably comes from an ancient nomadic legend, all the more remarkable since it appears in several medieval European tales, including that of King Arthur. The heroes of such stories lived during the fifth century A.D.—a period when nomads from the steppes poured into western Europe and perhaps inspired the cult of chivalry.

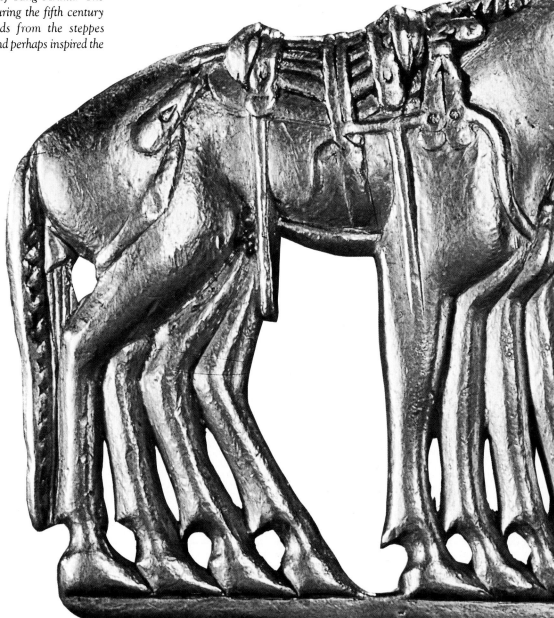

This superbly decorated glass cup was made for the Sarmatians—eastern neighbors of the Scythians—who loved to combine precious metals with colored stones. Gold filigree inlaid with garnets surrounds the vessel's rim, and hanging from it are chains ending in carnelians and gold balls. Invading Sarmatians displaced or absorbed the Scythians, who by the second century A.D.—the probable date of this treasure—had vanished as a distinct people.

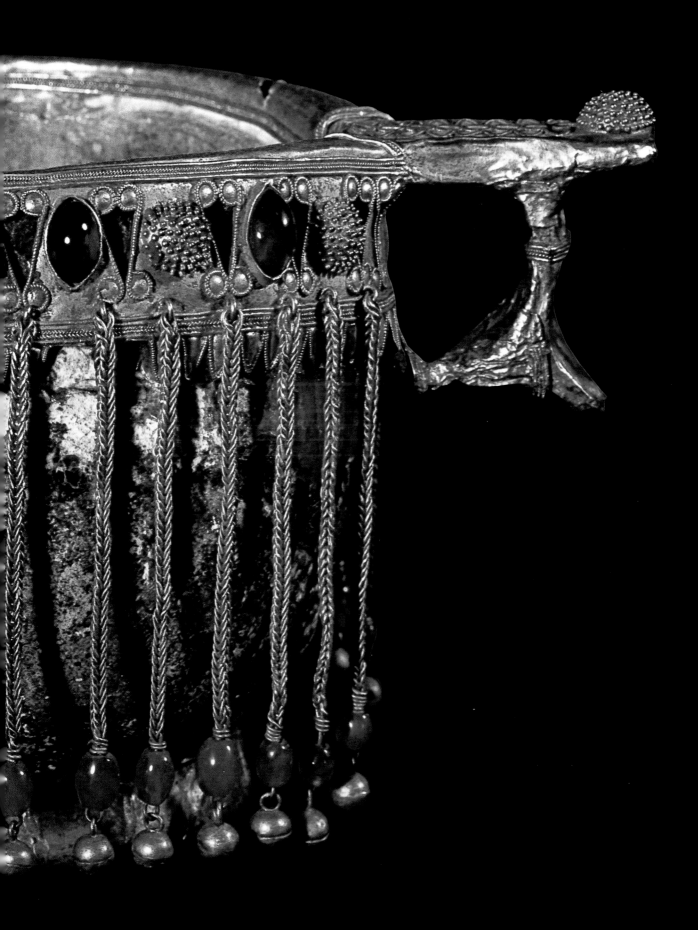

40

II

LEGENDS OF THE CELTS

AND THEIR SACRED GROVES

On leaving a battlefield, [the Celts] tie the heads of their enemies to their horse's neck, bring them home, and nail them as a showpiece on their doorways. . . . Heads of famous enemies they preserve in oil of cedar and display to visitors." So states the Greek geographer Strabo. He was describing a people who can be traced back in history at least as far as the seventh century B.C. and who, by the fifth and fourth, occupied a swath of Europe that reached from the upper Danube to Spain and Portugal, with out-riders in Britain and Ireland; a people who link east with west, who roamed over not only Europe but Asia Minor and the Near East, who challenged, in the third century B.C., the power of the Scythians and the Sarmatians on Russia's steppe. A Celtic tribe, the Parisi, gave its name to the capital of France; the Boii to Bohemia. They left their mark everywhere they went.

The Celts in Europe went in for human sacrifice as well as head-hunting. Julius Caesar reports this, and he would know: he fought the Celts of Gaul—modern France—for seven years, from 58 to

The enigmatic stone face at left, an image of a god or hero, was venerated in a Celtic sanctuary in what is now Czechoslovakia around the second century B.C.

51 B.C. What brought him there was the sad fact that, though one of Rome's most powerful politicians, he was penniless, and the quickest way to make a fortune in his day was through booty from conquered enemies. So he got himself appointed commander in chief of a long-term expedition against the Gauls. "All the Gauls," he says,

are totally dedicated to religious practices, and that is why any who fall sick or are involved in battle and danger use, or vow to use, human beings for their sacrificial victims. . . . It is their belief that, unless one human life is rendered for another, the immortal gods' anger cannot be soothed. They hold state sacrifices of this kind. Some Gauls have colossal human likenesses made of wicker whose arms and legs they fill with live men, set them on fire, and the men die engulfed in the flames. It is their belief that the immortal gods prefer the sacrificing of people caught in theft or highway robbery or other crimes, but, since this source of supply does not fill the need, they descend to sacrificing even the innocent.

For certain gods burning would not do; the victims had to be hanged or drowned. On a beautifully decorated silver bowl of the first century B.C., which, though found at Gundestrup in Denmark, was surely an import from some Celtic area, there is just such a ritual drowning portrayed.

"They use Druids to carry out the sacrifices," Caesar adds. The Druids were an order of priests who were especially powerful since the administration of law as well as religion was in their hands. Whoever had a quarrel, from lowly individuals to chieftains of mighty tribes, brought it to the Druids. The parties had to abide by the verdict on pain of exclusion from all sacrifices—a maximum sentence inasmuch as anybody so excluded became ritually unclean, not to be associated with, a pariah. Studying for the Druidhood took years, in some cases as many as twenty. Acolytes had to spend this much time in the long and arduous task of memorizing sacred verses, a task made necessary by the Druids' taboo against putting anything down in writing. No doubt in the Celts' earlier days when, like all barbarian peoples, they were illiterate, oral transmission was the only way to pass on information. But by Caesar's time they had adopted the Greek alphabet and had learned to write. The

The bronze statuette above, about five inches high, is a Roman artist's view of the fierce Celtic warrior, who sometimes fought naked except for a belt, a helmet, and a torque around the neck. The warrior is poised to hurl a spear, now lost.

Druids, however, insisted on following the age-old tradition.

There was something fierce and strange about the Celtic deities themselves as well as the sacrifices made to them. One powerful god, Tarvos Trigaranos, had the attributes of a bull. Another, Cernunnos, was horned. Epona was a goddess always connected with horses. Badb, a goddess of battle, was able to take the shape of a raven or crow. A goddess named Mórríghan, who appears in Irish literature, may be the forerunner of Morgan le Fay, the magic-working sister of King Arthur who, in one version of the legend, tried to kill him.

The Celts' places of worship were as forbidding as their deities and practices. The oak tree was sacred to them, and their preferred sanctuaries were dark groves hidden in deep forests. One near Marseilles, says the Roman poet Lucan, was amid trees that "from ancient times on had never been touched by human hand. Their interlaced branches, closing out the sun above, made the air dark and the shadows gelid. . . . Here gods were worshiped with barbaric rites; the altars were heaped with fell offerings, and every tree had been ritually cleansed with human gore." The "fell offerings" were human heads, for among the Celts these were an object of worship. They displayed severed heads not only on altars but on the facades of temples. These were simple structures of wood with thatched roofs, encircled by verandas for processions or sacred offerings or the like. The preferred decor was heads, some of them representations carved in stone or wood, but a good number actual heads.

Grisly votives were not the only kind dedicated in the sacred groves. The Celts deposited treasures there too, not only the booty warriors brought back from conquered enemies but also bulk gold and silver. Certain lakes were reckoned as sacred, and the Celts put treasure in them as well; it was safer resting on the bottom than in a grove. The amounts stored in these places were fabulous. A Greek writer of the first century B.C., Posidonius, reports that the treasure, gold and silver bullion, in the lakes and groves around what is today Toulouse, was worth fifteen thousand talents—a sum that not even kings and emperors could often command. After the Romans conquered Gaul, they auctioned off the sacred lakes, and many lucky

THE CULT OF THE HEAD

After a battle a victorious Celt often cut off the heads of the men he had slain—a custom that appalled the Romans, who assumed that the practice rose out of sheer thirst for gore. In fact, taking the heads of slain enemies sprang from deep religious conviction. The Celts believed that a person's head was his soul—the center of emotions and of life itself. Even after the body had died, a severed head retained its life-force in Celtic belief. Thus when a hero took the heads of his enemies, he took on their power as well. Nailed above the gates of a town or over the door of a warrior's house, heads brought good luck and kept evil at bay.

A Welsh tale illustrates the special magical powers of a severed head. A hero named Bran, wounded in a raid on Ireland, asked his comrades to lop off his head. They took the severed head to a great hall in the Otherworld— the life after death—where Bran's head entertained the company with feasts for eighty years. Later Bran's head was buried in London and protected the city from plague and conquest until someone dug it up.

In southern France the Celts erected two sanctuaries where they venerated human heads. At Roquepertuse, built in the third century B.C., six-foot-high pillars (right and in detail at left) held heads in niches. What rites the priests of Roquepertuse conducted no one knows; but the Roman historian Livy reported that at the most hallowed Celtic temples the priests cleaned the skulls of dead enemies, coated them with gold, and poured libations to the gods from these glittering, grisly trophies.

A HEAD IN ITS NICHE

THE SHRINE OF ROQUEPERTUSE

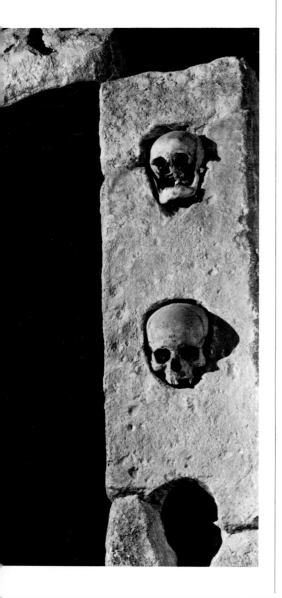

buyers hauled up masses of hammered silver as big as millstones.

The best place for the hunting of heads was the battlefield, and this is where Celtic men preferred to spend their time; "the whole race is war-mad," declared Strabo. They fought with spears and heavy iron swords, protecting themselves only with long wooden shields, though chieftains might wear helmets. Some did not even bother with shields: they fought stark naked, convinced that nudity magically kept them from harm. Young men were required by law to be in good trim; they were tested with a belt of a certain length, and all who had developed a potbelly and could not get it around them had to pay a fine. In emergencies women took the field to fight alongside the men—and formidably. One Roman historian reports that "a whole troop of strangers cannot take on any Gaul in a fight if his wife is with him. Much the stronger, fire in her eye, gnashing her teeth, she will begin to throw around those huge heavy arms of hers and, adding kicks from her feet, deliver blows like a catapult."

Another describes Queen Boadicea, who led the British Celts in a desperate revolt against Rome in A.D. 61, as "huge in body, absolutely terrifying in appearance, a deadly fierce look in her eye, a hoarse voice and a mass of hair, redder than red, down to her buttocks." The sight of tall, fair-skinned, blond or red-haired Celts, especially the husky Celtic women, obviously startled the small, dark Romans.

Both Greeks and Romans report in awed terms the bravery of Celtic women; they would kill their children sooner than see them enslaved by an enemy. They were, if anything, hardier than their mates. Strabo tells of a Celtic woman who, when hired along with a gang of men "to dig ditches...feeling pains, went off a little way from where she was working, gave birth, and came right back to the job in order not to lose her pay"—probably the earliest instance on record of that traditional mark of the rugged peasant woman. Celtic wives, not surprisingly, practiced couvade, the arrangement, still extant among some peoples today, whereby a woman who has had a baby leaves the bed and puts her husband in it and treats him as if he had been the one who went through labor.

Caesar's accounts of his campaigns against the Gauls are full of

TEXT CONTINUED ON PAGE 52

A WORLD OF
SEA AND STONE

For several centuries before Christ, groups of
Celts made their way from continental Europe to the shores of Ireland and gradually took
possession of that spectacularly verdant, fertile
land. Spared the depredations of Roman conquest, Ireland flowered, distinctly Celtic in language, arts, and ways—a world apart.

That world was rough and contentious. The
island was a patchwork of over one hundred
small kingdoms, allied into four large realms
that were often at odds with one another. Irish
sagas tell of a heroic age, dating roughly from the
second century B.C. to the fourth century A.D.,
when chariot-borne warriors battled over land
and women or simply for sport. A warrior's
boast, from the tale of a feud between the kingdoms of Ulster and Connacht, sums up the spirit
of the era: "I have never been a day without
having slain a Connachtman...."

As bellicose as the Irish were, they were always ready to put down their weapons in the
midst of a battle at the urging of a poet. For it was
one of the idiosyncrasies of the Celtic character
that they admired eloquence as highly as they
did a sturdy right arm. Under Irish law the
penalty for harming a poet was the same as that
for injuring a king.

Irish Christianity was equally idiosyncratic.
That lusty, pagan people readily adopted Christianity. Kings gave their land for churches and
monasteries, then plundered them. The monasteries even battled among themselves. The
church wealth that was at the root of these
troubles made some monks uneasy; they left the
comfort of the monasteries for the harsh solitude
and self-denial of barren, offshore islands such as
Great Skellig (pages 50–51).

*The Atlantic Ocean lashes the daunting cliffs of
Moher (right), seven hundred feet high. These cliffs
stretch five miles along Ireland's western coast—the
farthest limit of the Celtic world.*

A Celtic chieftain fortified his stronghold with a swath of jagged rocks (above) some time between the first and third centuries.

This defense work was one of several walls that protected an eleven-acre enclosure on Inishmore, the largest of the Aran Islands.

On a tiny island eight miles from shore, monks founded the monastery called Skellig Michael in the seventh or eighth

century. A simple oratory of stones (above) and a cross, which may mark the grave of a monk, look out over the sea.

The sandstone pillar above represents a god with the emblem of a boar on his chest. Revered by the Celts for their strength and ferocity, boars often appeared in Celtic art. This pillar probably stood in a sanctuary or household as an object of worship.

TEXT CONTINUED FROM PAGE 45

examples of the Celts' magnificent fighting spirit. Their finest hour came in 52 B.C. when Caesar had, as he thought, just about completed the pacification of Gaul. Suddenly he was confronted by a revolt that blazed up throughout the land. The cause was the appearance on the scene of a charismatic young Gaul named Vercingetorix.

His looks were impressive: very tall, and in a full suit of armor, he cut an imposing figure. But what counted far more were his indomitable will, his iron determination to resist the Romans at whatever cost, and his gift for communicating this determination to the various tribes of Gallic Celts, who had hitherto been interested more in fighting each other than the invaders. Luckily for the revolt Vercingetorix was an able commander as well as a fiery patriot. For the best part of a year he held his own against the man considered to be one of the great military geniuses of history.

And the moment came when it looked as if Vercingetorix had won the game: he had Caesar and all his forces in a trap from which there seemed to be no getting out. This was at Alesia, a walled Celtic town in Burgundy some thirty-five miles northwest of Dijon. Vercingetorix, considering the place impregnable, had locked himself up in it with eighty thousand men and called for help from all over Gaul. With probably little more than half that number, Caesar laid siege, ringing the wall with his men—and up came more than 250,000 Gauls to ring him in turn. Only the legions' magnificent discipline and Caesar's inspired generalship saved the day; he not only kept Vercingetorix from breaking out but smashed the relieving army.

To Caesar, Vercingetorix was a barbarian. Yet what happened next reveals the so-called civilized Roman as more barbaric than his opponent. Vercingetorix, in order to save the lives of his followers, offered to give himself up. It was a gallant gesture, and he carried it out gallantly. Plutarch reports the scene in his *Life of Caesar.* The young Gaul "dressed himself in his finest suit of armor, mounted his horse, and rode out through the gates [of Alesia]. He executed a complete circle around where Caesar was sitting, dismounted, stripped off his armor, and seated himself at Caesar's feet. There he remained motionless until handed over to be held under guard for the victory parade."

The victory parade, as it happened, did not take place until six years later. During all that time Vercingetorix languished in a Roman jail. Then, after his captors paraded him together with an Egyptian princess and a Tunisian prince and other samples of Rome's unconquerable might, they cavalierly put the Celtic hero to death.

———————————

Julius Caesar and his contemporaries were by no means the first Romans to tangle with the Celts. In the fifth century B.C. a horde of Celts from Gaul had climbed over the Alps and descended on Italy, taking over all of the north as far as Tuscany. About 390 B.C. a spearhead drove farther south, routed a powerful Roman army that tried to stop them a dozen miles north of Rome, and sacked the city thoroughly. A little over a century later, another restless group of Gauls, pushing down the Danube valley, burst into Greece and were halted just short of the celebrated sanctuary of Apollo at Delphi, whose precious votive offerings would have made rich pickings for the invaders. Three tribes elected to keep moving south. They smashed their way to Asia Minor, where they set up a state of their own called Galatia—*Galatoi* is Greek for "Gauls"—and spent most of their time ravaging their Greek neighbors. Eventually, by about 230 B.C., one of the Greek rulers in Asia Minor managed to build up a strong enough army to hold them in check. After that they gradually became assimilated, speaking Greek in addition to Celtic and slowly losing their traditional ways in favor of the Hellenic mode of life. Some of them became early converts to Christianity, the Galatians to whom St. Paul addressed a famous epistle.

But the vast majority of Celts, living in the western part of the ancient world, were absorbed into Roman rather than Greek civilization. Those in north Italy were the first, having succumbed to Roman arms by 200 B.C. By 50 B.C. Caesar had completed his conquest of Gaul; on his heels there flooded in Roman administra-

This statue of a robed Druid was part of a cache the Celts buried at a sanctuary on the Loire in the first century B.C., perhaps to keep it out of Roman hands. The Druid may be gesturing at a rite or haranguing warriors before a battle.

A Celtic chief named Coviomarus struck the silver coin above in the first century B.C. The worn image still shows the spiky hairdo of the Celts, who washed their hair with lime and formed it into sharp points, stiff enough to impale an apple.

tors, soldiers, colonists, and tradesmen. Their presence set in motion an irresistible process that ended up converting Gaul into the most thoroughly Romanized of all the areas under Rome's domination. The Gauls gave up human sacrifice and head-hunting. The Gallic gods became fused with Roman deities, the Celtic languages gave way to Latin, Druid law to Roman law, Celtic villages to Roman-style towns complete with forum, baths, and amphitheaters. Similar Romanization went on in Spain and Britain.

In one place, however, the Celts were able to carry on undisturbed—Ireland. The island was by no means beyond the ken of the Greeks and Romans. They knew the names of the Celtic tribes that lived there and the names of their larger towns. They were aware that Ireland was extraordinarily green, to judge by the report of Pomponius Mela, a geographer who wrote in the first century A.D. Irish pasture, he says, was so luxuriant that cattle had to be carefully watched; otherwise they ate so much they burst. Solinus, a geographer of the third century A.D., even knew that there were no snakes on the island.

Rome never sent her legions against this remote corner of the ancient world. The Celts there were not only able to go their own way but, when the appropriate time came, to undertake conquests of their own. As Rome's hold on Britain began to weaken, they were swift to take advantage of the situation: by the third century A.D., Irish Celts were moving into Wales, by the fifth the Scotti—the name is from an Irish verb, "to raid"—into northern Britain.

Ireland, as a consequence, was the one place where Celtic culture was able to attain full flower. Here the Celtic language never gave way to a conqueror's; here Celtic legend lived on to contribute to world literature the story of the star-crossed love of Tristram and Isolt; the sorrows of the pathetic Deirdre; the feats of the dark-haired Cuchulain, the warrior-hero of the Irish saga, *Táin Bó Cualnge*. Here Christianity, under the Celtic touch, inspired artists to create church objects of surpassing beauty—sculpture, unique jewels, and masterpieces of manuscript illumination that remain among the great treasures of the Western world.

THE REALM
OF DREAMS

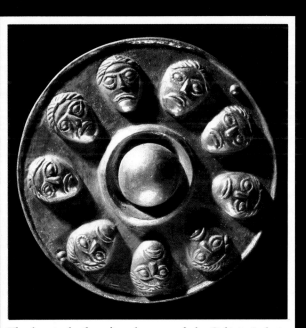

The four-inch silver disc above, made by Celts in Italy in the second century B.C., ornamented a horse's harness. The images of heads warded off evil from horse and rider.

By about 300 B.C. the Celts had much of Europe in their hands. From the Black Sea to Ireland, Celtic tribes held some 800,000 square miles of land. They had already invaded Italy, plundering Rome itself in 390 B.C., and would soon launch a devastating expedition against Greece. Aristotle held them up as an example of foolhardy fearlessness, and other classical writers labeled the Celts boastful, "unbearable in victory," and vain. The sight of triumphant Celtic warriors strutting in their imposing helmets, similar to the horned and conical headgear on pages 62–63, and sporting heavy gold torques such as the one on pages 60–61, no doubt irritated the apprehensive Greek or Roman observer.

Though no strong man ever rose up to weld the far-flung Celtic tribes into an empire, all the Celts shared a common culture. They were united in language, religion, and art. The treasures of the Celts reveal aspects of their complex character: clever and refined, yet superstitious and preoccupied with the eerie. Strange animals perch atop the flagon at left. Images of monsters and grim-faced gods decorate the caldron on pages 66–71. On the shield on pages 64–65, disembodied staring eyes appear and disappear, as in a dream or in a world where magic reigns. In these objects can be found the inscrutability that a Greek writer noted in the way the Celts talked: "They speak in riddles...hinting at things and leaving much to be understood."

The intensity and vitality of the Celts was scarcely dimmed when they relinquished paganism for Christianity. Their vigorous if uncanny spirit expressed itself in the treasures wrought for Ireland's monasteries, such as the simple yet splendid Ardagh Chalice on pages 78–79 and the beautiful shrine on pages 80–81, which preserved the bones of an Irish saint.

A chief in the prosperous salt-mining region near Dürrnberg in Austria was buried with the bronze wine flagon at left about 400 B.C. At the top of the handle a monster devours a human head, flanked by long-tailed beasts, with the limbs of half-eaten victims in their mouths. The base of the handle, in detail opposite, terminates in another human head, surrounded by an abstract design of linked curves.

This graceful arch of gold (above), a diadem worn over the hair, belonged to a princess of the sixth century B.C. At each end of the ornament a winged horse (detail, opposite)—perhaps Pegasus of Greek mythology—prances on delicate filigree. The diadem was an import from far-off Greece and bespeaks the wealth and power of the princess, who lived near strongholds that probably controlled the tin trade on the Seine River.

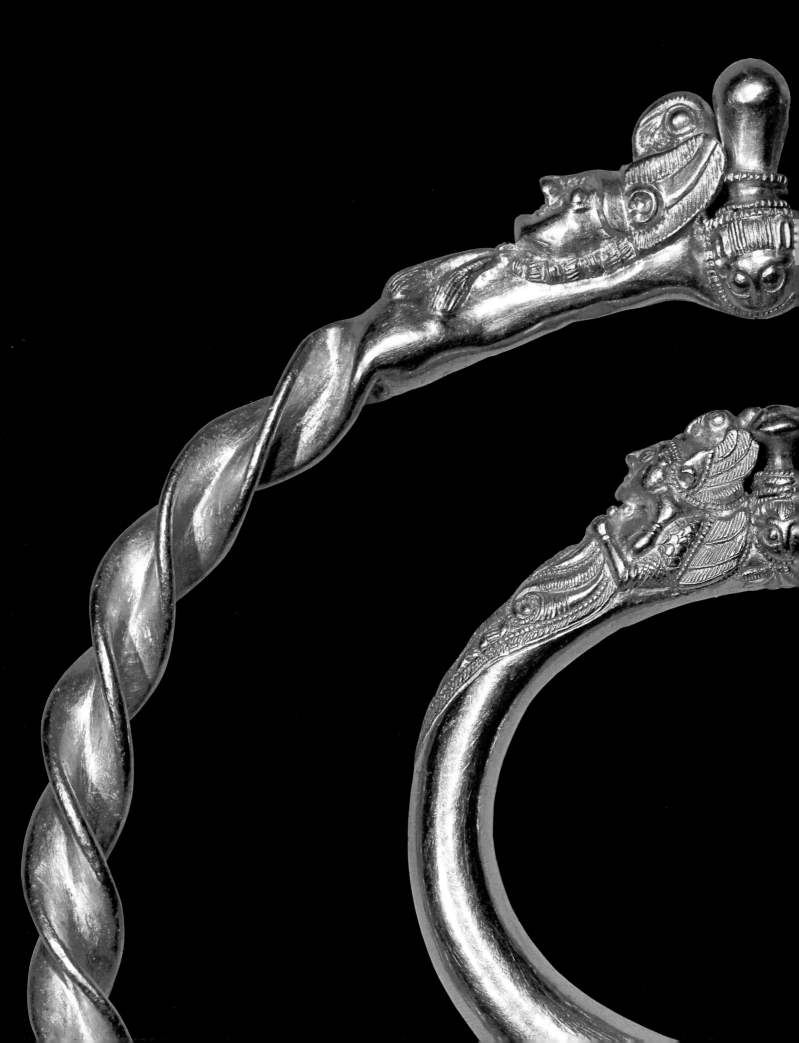

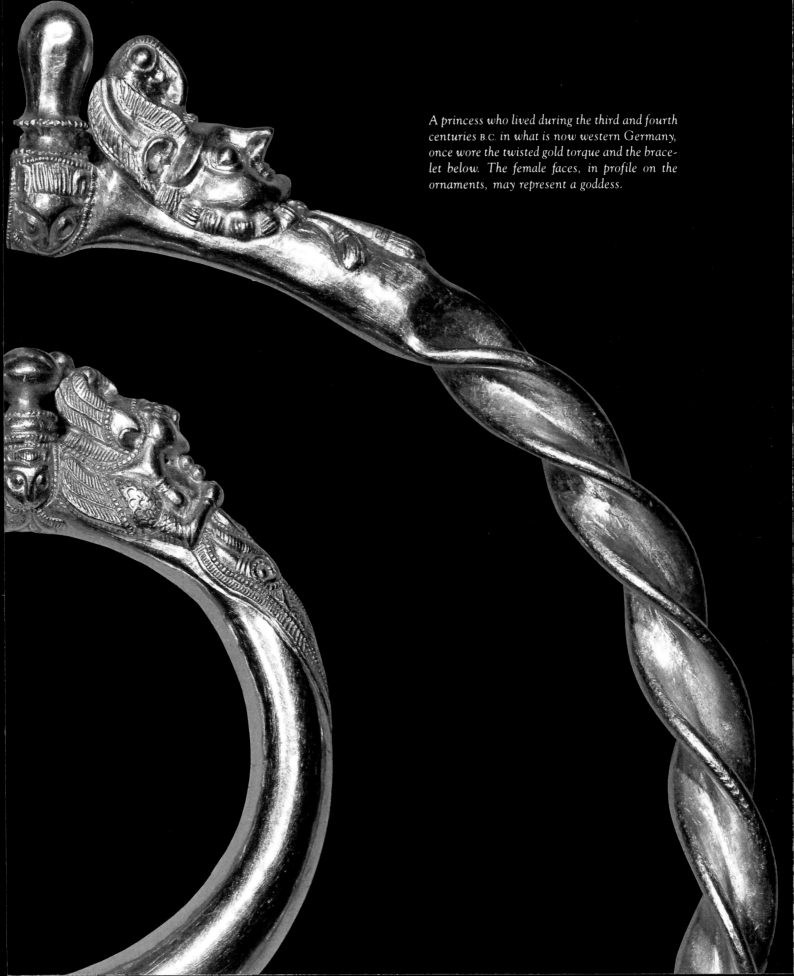

A princess who lived during the third and fourth centuries B.C. in what is now western Germany, once wore the twisted gold torque and the bracelet below. The female faces, in profile on the ornaments, may represent a goddess.

A chieftain rode into battle wearing the fifteen-inch-high conical helmet at left, found in a fifth-century-B.C. grave in northern France. A piece of coral, imported from the Mediterranean, decorates the medallion on the visor.

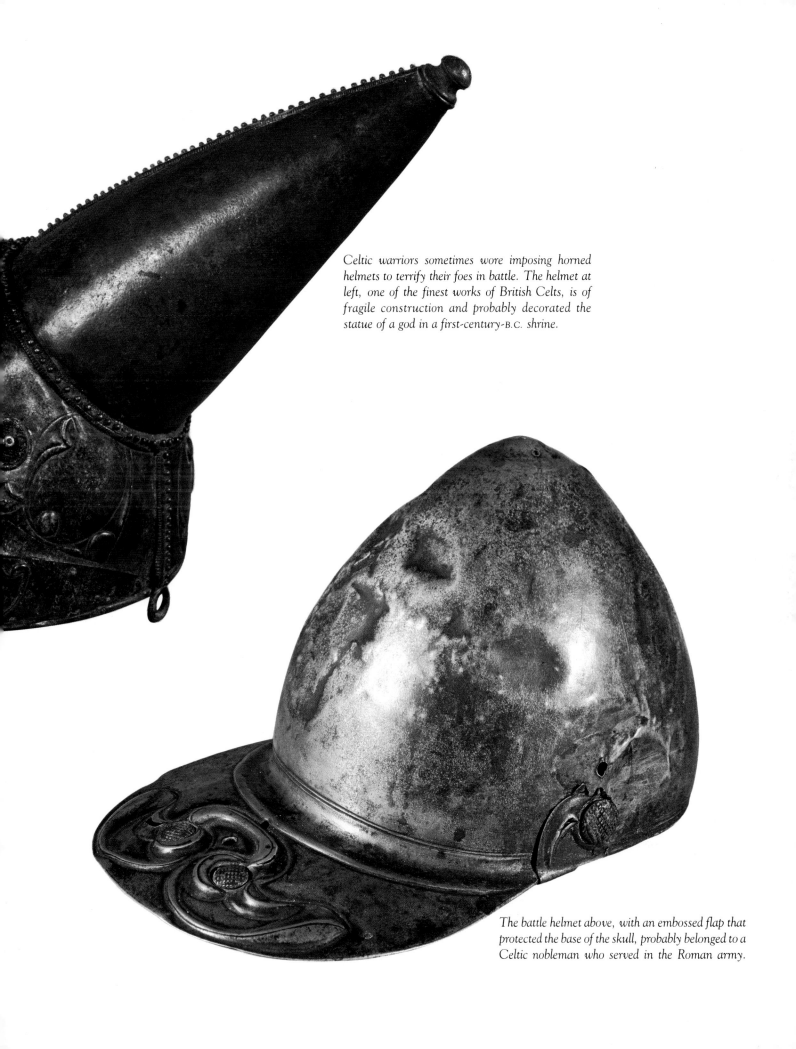

Celtic warriors sometimes wore imposing horned helmets to terrify their foes in battle. The helmet at left, one of the finest works of British Celts, is of fragile construction and probably decorated the statue of a god in a first-century-B.C. shrine.

The battle helmet above, with an embossed flap that protected the base of the skull, probably belonged to a Celtic nobleman who served in the Roman army.

A lively bestiary swarms across these two panels of the Gundestrup caldron. Winged griffins and leopards (above) prance around a bearded god and his attendant, who wears a helmet with ox horns and holds a wheel—perhaps a symbol of the sun

A Celtic chief threw the bronze shield at right—once backed with leather or wood—into the Thames as an offering to the river god in the first century A.D. One of the great masterworks of Celtic craftsmanship, the shield is embossed with delicate curving ornamentation and studded with colored enamel. Some of the enamel designs may be outlines of highly stylized animals. The circles in the detail opposite, for example, could be the brooding eyes of an owl.

Twelve embossed panels formed the Gundestrup caldron, here reconstructed.

Caldrons were sacred vessels to the Celts. At rites Druids filled them with potions made from mistletoe and other plants believed to give health and fertility. At sacrifices caldrons caught the blood of human victims, and the Celts also regarded them as symbols of plenty.

The Gundestrup caldron (above), named for the town in Denmark near which it was found in 1891, is the most magnificent Celtic caldron ever found—a supreme work of silversmithing and a treasure that may well have been the most precious sacred object in the entire Celtic world in the first century B.C.

The caldron, twenty-seven inches wide, was probably made in southeastern Europe for a Celtic tribe that prized silver above gold. The scenes on the panels (see foldout) narrate mythological events in symbols only a priest could interpret. How the caldron found its way to distant Denmark is a mystery. A marauding Celtic tribe may have carried it off as war booty.

At some time in the first century B.C., perhaps in the midst of a political crisis, a chief in need of divine aid offered the caldron to the gods. Priests dismantled it and left the panels in a neat heap on the ground—an offering so hallowed that no one dared to plunder it. Eventually the peat bog on which it lay swallowed it up.

FOLDOUT⟶

Cernunnos, a horned god who was lord of the animals, presides over the panel above, clutching a magical torque in one hand and a ram-headed snake in the other. At upper right, a man rides on a sea creature that may be a Mediterranean dolphin.

A god, whose severe face once glowered with glass eyes, grasps sacrificial stags on a panel that retains some of its original gilt.

The third-century-B.C. bronze sculpture above is an appliqué, originally attached to a wooden pitcher with nails driven through the holes that are visible in several places on the piece. The openwork below the animal's head decorated the body of the pitcher, and the horns above the head cradled the neck of the vessel. The animal (detail, opposite) may be an Asian ibex or a bull.

74

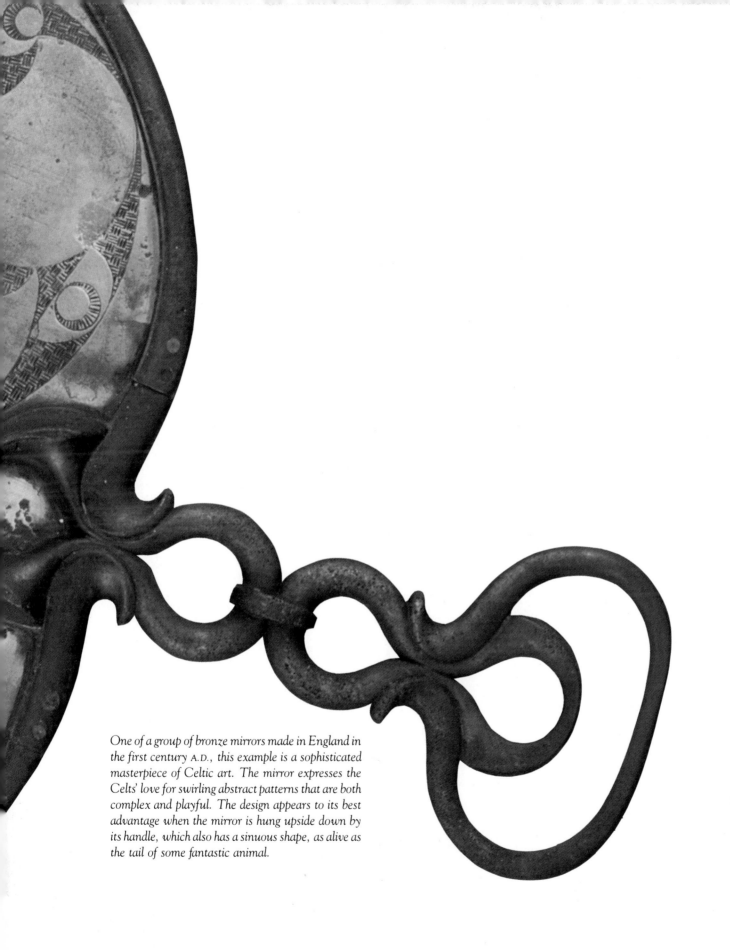

One of a group of bronze mirrors made in England in the first century A.D., this example is a sophisticated masterpiece of Celtic art. The mirror expresses the Celts' love for swirling abstract patterns that are both complex and playful. The design appears to its best advantage when the mirror is hung upside down by its handle, which also has a sinuous shape, as alive as the tail of some fantastic animal.

An eighth-century Irish noble once fastened his cloak with the spectacular brooch at right—the apex of Celtic artistry in metal. On the semicircular band at the top edge of the brooch, four serpents writhe with their heads and tails projecting over the edge. Other serpents twine around each other in a highly intricate pattern on the roughly square panel bordered by six amber beads. In the two flanking panels, whirling circles of silver inlaid with copper echo the contortions of the snakes. The unknown maker wrought these subtle and elaborate decorations on a brooch that is but three inches wide.

ARDAGH CHALICE

An Irish artist made the silver chalice above, found buried near the town of Ardagh, in the eighth century A.D., to hold wine during the celebration of the Mass. The names of eleven disciples—Judas has been left out—and St. Paul are inscribed against a stippled background around the middle of the chalice. Beneath both handles are escutcheons, opposite, with studs of colored glass and delicate lacings of gold wire, topped with tiny granules of gold.

OVERLEAF: This wooden shrine, over a foot and a half high, was made in the twelfth century to hold relics of a seventh-century Irish saint. After robbers stripped off a decorative layer of silver, the monks who owned the shrine added fifty standing bronze figures, of which eleven remain. Copied from statues in continental Europe, the figures are crude compared to the lively Celtic ornamentation on the edges and on the central cross.

III

THREE AGAINST ROME

ALARIC, ATTILA, AND THEODORIC

I n 390 B.C. the Celts of Gaul sacked Rome. Thereafter the Romans became so powerful that for centuries they never feared attack—and for eight hundred years never suffered any until, in A.D. 409, a barbarian king at the head of a rough and tough army encamped before the walls. This was Alaric, chieftain of a Germanic tribe that until recently had lived along the Danube River. The Romans sent out a pair of high-ranking envoys to negotiate; these came back with nothing more substantial than samples of Alaric's sardonic sense of humor. They had started with bluster: if he attacked he would be met, they assured him, by innumerable hosts. "The thicker the hay, the easier mowed," he observed with a guffaw. They changed their tune and asked him to name his price, which turned out to be all the gold and silver, every slave of barbarian origin, and every bit of movable property in the city. "What will that leave us?" they asked in despair. "Your lives," was the grim reply.

For many it did not leave even that. In his magisterial *Decline and Fall of the Roman Empire*, the great eighteenth-century English

Leovigild, on horseback, a sixth-century Visigothic king of Spain, executes a rebel chieftain. The ivory carving is from an eleventh-century Spanish reliquary.

The grim ferocity of Attila is evident in the medallion above, which an Italian sculptor carved centuries after the Hunnish king's death in the fifth century. Though Attila had a chance to loot Rome, the pleas of a pope turned him back.

historian Edward Gibbon eloquently described the sequel. "The trembling senate," he wrote,

without any hopes of relief, prepared, by a desperate resistance, to delay the ruin of their country. But they were unable to guard against the secret conspiracy of their slaves and domestics; who, either from birth or interest, were attached to the cause of the enemy. At the hour of midnight, the Salarian gate was silently opened, and the inhabitants were awakened by the tremendous sound of the Gothic trumpet. Eleven hundred and sixty-three years after the foundation of Rome, the Imperial city, which had subdued and civilized so considerable a part of mankind, was delivered to the licentious fury of the tribes of Germany and Scythia.

Alaric's men broke into Rome on August 24, 410, through the gate where the Via Salaria, one of the main roads from the north, met the city wall. To find their way in the dark, they set fire to the houses that flanked the street leading in from the gate. For six days the king let them kill and loot and rape. Forty thousand slaves took advantage of the situation to run out on their masters and join in the destruction. There were a few bright spots in the dismal picture. Alaric, for example, gave strict orders to his forces to keep their hands off the churches of St. Peter and of St. Paul. And on occasion the men needed no orders. A raging Gothic band came upon an aged virgin with a hoard of precious plate; they let her alone when she told them, "These are the consecrated vessels belonging to St. Peter; if you presume to touch them, the sacrilegious deed will remain on your conscience." Word of what had happened came to the king. He commanded that the objects all be brought to the Vatican; and so they were, in a formal parade of Gothic soldiers loaded down with vessels of gold and silver.

The rampaging Goths whom Alaric led were a branch of the great federation of Germanic tribes, sharing a common Teutonic tongue and inhabiting northern Europe east of the Rhine. By peaceable agreement with the Romans, this branch—the Visigoths, or western

Goths—had in about A.D. 275 settled along the Danube River in the Carpathian Mountains. To the east in the Black Sea region lived their kinsmen the Ostrogoths, or eastern Goths. Like all the Germanic tribes, the Goths were redoubtable fighters, redoubtable enough to withstand triumphantly the Romans' attempts to conquer them. In 58 B.C. Caesar had come into contact with some of the tribes during his campaigns in Gaul. His army at the time was still new to warfare with barbarian warriors; when tales began to circulate of the size, strength, and ferocity of the Germanic brand, his men took such fright they started drawing up their wills. Although Caesar managed to rout all the German armies he faced, he was well aware of how formidable they were. "[Germans] spend all their time in hunting and war," he wrote. "From the time they are little children, they exercise at enduring labor and hardship." Young men, he reported, even held off from having sexual relations until they were twenty; this helped, they were convinced, "their growth, strength, and sinews." War was the be-all and end-all of a German male's existence. One particular tribe did not allow a youth to shave until he had killed a man in battle. "Many young aristocrats," declared the Roman historian Cornelius Tacitus, who in A.D. 98 published an essay on the Germans, "if their native state is stagnating in a long peace...of their own accord seek out tribes that are carrying on some war."

Theodoric the Great, the Ostrogothic ruler of Italy from 493 until 526, holds a symbol for victory on the gold solidus, or Roman coin, above. It is inscribed in Latin Rex Theodoricus Pius Princis: *"King Theodoric, pious prince."*

If a chieftain fell in battle, his followers were obligated to fight on to the death. "To leave a battle alive," Tacitus explains, "after a chief has fallen, means infamy and disgrace for the rest of a man's life." Also, Germans fought with their families nearby, so they "could hear the shrieks of the women, the wailing of the infants"—a pressing form of encouragement, for women had great influence in German society. According to Tacitus the Germanic male "believes that there is in women something holy, some ability to foresee; he never scorns their advice or disregards their replies."

The Germans shared with the Celts a highly developed taste for war. They shared other tastes as well. They, too, favored gloomy groves as the appropriate setting for religious rites. They, too, practiced human sacrifice. One set of tribes, for example, kept a sacred chariot in a particular grove; they believed that in the cult ceremony an invisible goddess rode around in it. Afterward the chariot had to be ritually cleansed in a sacred lake by a gang of slaves who, when their job was finished, were duly drowned in the lake. Prisoners of war could end up as sacrifices on the altars. In A.D. 9 a group of German tribes ended any ideas the Romans had of subjugating them. They ambushed the Romans in a thick forest and utterly destroyed a powerful army. Of the few prisoners they took, they sacrificed the high ranking in the forest groves.

Yet, in certain ways, the Germans were very different from the Celts. The Celts were efficient farmers; the Germans left their farms in the hands of the women, the weak, and the elderly. The Celts built up villages and towns; the Germans preferred to live in widely separated homesteads. The Celts showed no great favor to their women; the Germans treated theirs with the highest regard. "They are," claims Tacitus, "almost alone among the barbarians to be content with a single wife." And the husband, not the wife, brought a dowry to the marriage. In return husbands insisted upon strict chastity. If a man caught his wife in adultery, he cut off her hair, stripped her naked, and flogged her. The Celts decked themselves with jewelry, wore brightly colored clothes, and laid their dead away in rich and well-marked tombs. The Germans dressed in only cloaks—"it was the mark of great wealth to have underwear," says Tacitus—and cremated their dead with scant ceremony or expense.

Next to fighting, Tacitus reports, German men most enjoyed hunting, drinking, and shooting dice, particularly the last. So seriously did they take it that they played—"surprisingly," comments Tacitus—only when sober. Another German custom was their method for getting prophecies. It involved horses—ritually pure, white horses maintained at public expense in sanctuaries and never ridden or put to drawing vehicles except for a sacred chariot. A priest or king would yoke them up to this, walk beside them, and tell the future from their neighs and snorts.

No Roman legions, after the disaster in A.D. 9, ventured to go after

Roman soldiers force Germanic tribesmen to decapitate their own men—a grisly end to the barbarians' raid on Italy about A.D. 170. This relief is from a stone column the emperor Marcus Aurelius raised in Rome to commemorate the bloody victory.

the Germans in their trackless retreats. Indeed the Romans concentrated on keeping these formidable warriors from coming after them. The emperors ordered the construction of a series of forts and strong points, in places an actual wall, along the frontier to fence off Rome's enticingly rich lands and towns from barbarian territory. It was a line of defense, not a line to close off contact; there was plenty of contact. Roman traders circulated freely, exchanging bronzeware and silverware—bowls, cups, dishes—for amber, hides, furs. In the course of time, the Germans became well aware that, over the border, life was a good deal fuller and easier than in their gloomy woodlands. What is more, the Roman government was willing to pay for what the Germans cheerfully did for pleasure—fighting.

Roman citizens, whose taste for peace in this age ran as strongly as the Germans' did for war, were increasingly reluctant to serve as soldiers, and Roman commanders were forever on the lookout for likely recruits. Germanic youths flooded south to sign up and were so welcome that by the fourth century A.D. they were the backbone of Rome's armed forces. The emperor's elite guard at Constantinople was totally Germanic. Most of the officer staff, including generals, were Germanic. As a consequence when the mighty movement of the Goths, the easternmost of the Germanic tribes, got under way about A.D. 375—the movement that was to shove the Roman Empire into the initial stages of its decline and fall—the troops opposing them were largely their own kinsmen. Roman civilization was both attacked and defended by barbarians.

Alaric did not long survive his epoch-making sack of Rome. Before the year was out he had died, and his army of Visigoths left Italy to concentrate their destructive attention on France and Spain. Rome's relief, however, was short-lived. Within a few decades she faced another threat, this time from the notorious Attila, the "scourge of God." He was a leader not of Germans but of Huns— hard-bitten, hard-riding Mongols who had galloped out of central Asia to sweep over eastern Europe, destroying, pillaging, and driving people into a headlong rush to escape death or enslavement. Pressure from the Huns was what had set the Visigoths moving southward until they eventually invaded the rich fields of Italy and, under Alaric, sacked Rome. The next invaders were the Huns themselves, even more fearsome, with Attila at their head.

Here is Gibbon's description of him as translated from the Latin of Jordanes, a writer on Gothic history: "a large head, a swarthy complexion, small, deep-seated eyes, a flat nose, a few hairs in the place of a beard, broad shoulders, and a short square body of nervous strength though of a disproportioned form. The haughty step and demeanour of the king of the Huns expressed the consciousness of his superiority above the rest of mankind, and he had the custom of fiercely rolling his eyes as if he wished to enjoy the terror which he inspired."

Attila's power over his people was absolute. Standing at the door of his hut, he would hear whatever quarrels they had with each other and casually deliver offhand judgment—judgment from which there was no appeal. The vast amounts of treasure that, through looting and blackmail, fell into the hands of the Huns was all turned over to him. He astutely lavished great amounts on his more powerful followers—gold and silver plate, silver goblets and trays, bridles studded with gold and gems, Chinese silks, Indian pearls—and kept little for himself. This was not because he was an ascetic, for he had no hesitation in adopting many luxurious Roman ways in place of those of his primitive forefathers: he covered his bed with fine linen, dined in the Roman fashion reclining on a couch, took wine as his drink. On the other hand at meals he was ostentatiously old-fashioned. Guests at his banquets were served food on plates of silver and wine in silver goblets; he took his in plates and goblets of wood. They got the full range of Roman cuisine; he ate only meat.

In 441 this fierce-eyed master of sacking and slaving trained his sights on the Romans, beginning with those nearest him, in the east. Half a century earlier the Roman Empire had broken in two, the western part ruled by an emperor residing at different times in Ravenna, Rome, and Milan, and the eastern part ruled by an

STILICHO THE VANDAL AS ROMAN GENERAL

A FIFTH-CENTURY VANDAL NOBLEMAN

A LEGACY OF DESTRUCTION

For eighty years a barbaric tribe so terror-ized Gaul, Spain, and North Africa that its name came to denote wanton lawlessness. The Vandals, orginally from northern Jut-land, trampled through more territory than any other Germanic people, but left behind little more than a reputation for ruthlessness.

Initially some Vandals were adaptable to Roman ways and causes. One Vandal strong man, Stilicho, in the fourth-century ivory re-lief opposite, commanded the western Roman army for over a decade, defending Italy against the Visigoths. This barbarian became an im-perial hero, his statue raised in the Forum in Rome. Stilicho, however, was eventually ex-ecuted by ungrateful Romans on suspicion of

treason, and his fellow Vandals, still in Ger-many, were anything but champions of the Empire. Having reached the Rhine these ma-rauders shot through Gaul with the Huns at their heels and in 409 finally crossed the Pyrenees into Spain. For a time the Vandals held their own in southern Spain against the Romans and the Visigoths, but eventually de-cided to move on.

Looking south the Vandals' shrewd leader, Gaiseric, turned his army into a navy and crossed the Strait of Gibraltar to North Af-rica, the breadbasket of the Roman Empire. Storming eastward the Vandals took imperial outposts dotting the African coast until, at Carthage, they established their own capital.

With a hold on grain supplies, the Vandals kept the Romans in need and returned to sea as pirates, taking trade vessels on the Mediter-ranean and plundering Sicily and southern Italy. The looters amassed treasures that were never of their own making; the gold, jewels, mosaics, and sculptures they most coveted were Roman.

Living on large estates in North Africa, the pirate Vandals enjoyed the luxurious life and, like the nobleman in the mosaic above, lost some of their zeal for mindless raiding. In-creasingly disorganized under the uninspired successors to Gaiseric, the Vandals failed to resist a Roman attack in 533 and disappeared, having vandalized two continents.

An armed Visigothic knight displays his fearsome antler-style headdress as he bestrides his specially outfitted horse—only the most privileged warrior could hang bells from his saddle and harness. This miniature and the one opposite illustrate a twelfth-century Spanish manuscript.

emperor in Constantinople. Attila had been receiving 700 pounds of gold annually from Constantinople to keep the peace; he advanced, smashed a Roman army sent out to stop him, and forthwith raised the ante to 2,100 pounds with an additional 6,000 payable just to start things off properly. Rome could not stand such financial bloodletting very long. Luckily at this juncture Attila turned his attention to France. But there an army of Visigoths and Romans, joining forces to oppose a common enemy, brought him to a halt; so he made for Italy.

He ravaged the north and was preparing to do the same to the rest of the peninsula when a famous summit meeting wrought a dramatic change in the Hunnish king's plans. Attila was camped near Mantua. In 457 Pope Leo the Great traveled all the way from Rome to hold a parley. At the end of it the Huns made an abrupt about-face and left the country. No one knows what the pope said to Attila. Contemporaries believed that the apostles Peter and Paul had appeared to Attila and struck the fear of God in him with their threats. Modern historians suggest that Leo simply pointed out to Attila that plague was raging in Italy.

Within a year after this event Attila met his death, not gloriously on the battlefield but ingloriously in his marriage bed. It happened when he took, as the last in a series of wives, a beautiful young German girl. Ater the wedding the tippling went on and on, and it was very late before he finally staggered off to go to sleep. The next day, when hour after hour passed without his making an appearance, his servants decided to investigate. They broke into his chamber—to find the bride weeping over the corpse of her husband. He had had a heavy nosebleed—an ailment he often suffered from—and in his drunken state had suffocated.

His faithful Huns buried him with full honors. They erected a silk tent to shelter his remains and galloped round and round it to give their late commander a last display of the skill they had so long exercised in his behalf. They laid his body in a triple sarcophagus, one each of gold, silver, and iron; the first two symbolized the treasure he had taken from his enemies, the third the means by which he had taken it. Then they transferred the body from the tent to its burial mound and alongside it laid the arms Attila had stripped from conquered foes, as well as gems and other precious objects. The last step was to slaughter those who had carried this out and put their corpses beside his. The account comes from an eyewitness: the tomb remains hidden yet.

The menace of the Huns vanished after the death of their noted commander, and the Germans returned to the spotlight of history. The invasion of Italy that came to a climax with the sack of Rome had been the work of the Visigoths, those Germans who, until dislodged by the Huns, had lived in the lands beyond the Danube. The next invasion was mounted by their eastern cousins, the Ostrogoths, who, until they too yielded to the pressure of the Huns, had occupied south Russia.

In 474 a prince named Theodoric became king of the Ostrogoths. He was barely out of his teens but, despite his youth, circumstances had made him far more knowledgeable in the ways of civilized peoples than any of his roughhewn tribesmen. For, when Theodoric was only seven or eight years of age, his father had sent him off to the Roman emperor at Constantinople as a hostage; the emperor, having paid the Ostrogoths three hundred pounds of gold to sign them up as allies, wanted some guarantee that he would get his money's worth. At the court Theodoric drank up all the military learning he could but apparently not any other kind. He never, for example, learned to write; the future monarch of Italy signed his royal decrees with a mark and not a signature. After ten years the emperor was finally convinced of the Goths' good faith and sent Theodoric home. Not long after, his father died, and he took the crown.

For the next fourteen years Theodoric accomplished little, spending his time in fruitless warfare—at times for the Romans, at times against them, at times against rivals for his throne. Then in 488 he embarked on the expedition that was to gain him his place in history: with 100,000 of his people behind him, he invaded Italy. Five years later the peninsula was all his; the heartland of the Roman Empire had become an Ostrogothic state ruled by King Theodoric—

Invincible in his suit of iron mail, a whiskered foot soldier of the Visigothic army holds a long pike, a shield, and a double-edged sword. The infantryman's head-to-toe armor includes a conical helmet and nasal piece, a scaly sheath, guards for his legs, and metal-reinforced sandals.

Recceswinth, the Visigothic ruler of Spain from 653 to 672, holds a scroll, probably to signify his faith in Christianity as Muslims invaded the peninsula. The fine robes and diadem befit a civilized king, no longer a tough Germanic tribesman. This portrait is from a codex made by Spanish scribes in 976.

and he ruled it well. As Gibbon says, "It was the policy of Theodoric to disguise the reign of a Barbarian...a Gothic prince who had penetration to discern, and firmness to pursue, his own and the public interest."

He died in 526 and was buried in a massive stone mausoleum that still stands outside of Ravenna.

When Tacitus wrote, the Germans were simply barbarians with no taste for finery. They wore the plainest of garments and avoided ostentatious adornment. But by the fifth century, after flooding into the territories of the Roman Empire, they had ample occasion to observe the ways of the Roman aristocracy, a thin upper crust of owners of vast estates who lived in the most opulent splendor. The Germans not only learned of such ways but achieved the means to attain them, thanks to the loot from the towns they overran and the blackmail they levied upon the treasury of Rome.

Some were fabulously rich. A king in Gaul who betrothed his daughter to a Visigothic prince in Spain was able to send her off with fifty carriages loaded down with gold bullion, jewels, and costly garments. The procession never reached Spain; everybody helped themselves to the girl's precious belongings, from the very escort that was supposed to guard them to the unscrupulous rulers through whose territories she had to pass. Incidents like this explain why only the barest fraction of all the wealth of the Germans of these times has survived: some crown jewels, a few church donations, a scattering of personal adornments.

By the end of the fifth century A.D., the map of western Europe had changed radically. For centuries it had been part of the Roman Empire. Now Spain belonged to the Visigoths, France to the Germanic tribes called the Franks, Italy to the Ostrogoths. The line that for so long had fenced off the barbarians was no more. Celts, Franks, Visigoths, Ostrogoths—all had given up the ways of their forefathers for the ways of the Romans. In doing so they laid the foundations of medieval Europe.

BURNING
FOR GOLD

*This garnet-eyed peacock of soldered and granulated gold
may have studded the belt of a Hunnish warrior. Red glass
and additional garnets form the bird's beak and plumage.*

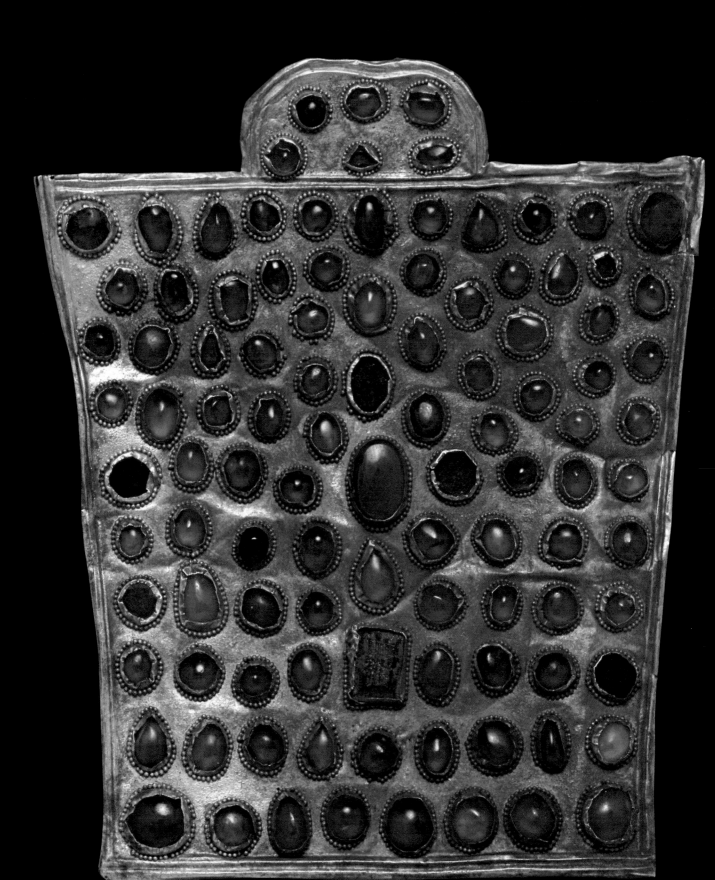

Though few barbarian chiefs at first displayed great wealth, the Germanic Goths and the Asiatic Huns clashing on the fringe of the Roman Empire by the fourth and fifth centuries A.D. were "burning for gold," in the words of a contemporary observer. The Visigoths, Ostrogoths, and Huns carried off the luxuries of the imperial cities until the burden of their riches slowed them down. Like most barbarian treasures, those of the Germanic tribes and the Huns were portable, chiefly jewelry and the lightweight gear of mounted warriors. Their prized possessions were not only the things they looted, but also the beautiful works of their own metalsmiths and jewelers. Hunnish, Visigothic, and Ostrogothic goldsmiths were particularly adept at soldering together delicate sheets of gold, granulating the metal, and studding it with stones (the larger the gem, the better). Sapphires, carnelians, garnets, a kind of garnet called almandine, and chips of colored glass went into the jewelry of the Huns and the Visigoths—and onto the elaborate bridles of their horses. The Ostrogoths were masters of fine inlay.

In Spain and Italy the Visigoths and Ostrogoths became Christians and paid homage to the Church with donations of crowns and crosses of gold. Hunnish and Gothic kings took pendants, brooches, and necklaces to their graves. The treasures on these and the following pages show that the Germanic and Asiatic tribes, made up of people who began as simple nomads, acquired an appetite for and an ability to make sophisticated jewelry, reserving the masterpieces of gold for their kings.

A warrior's leather whip fit into the golden cylinder at right, which is set with carnelians. A fourth-century Hunnish jeweler made the handle, trimming each end with twisted gold wires.

The gem-studded gold plaque opposite is the chamfron, or headpiece, for the horse of a fourth-century Hunnish chief. Beads of gold encircle carnelians and other gemstones—over one hundred in number.

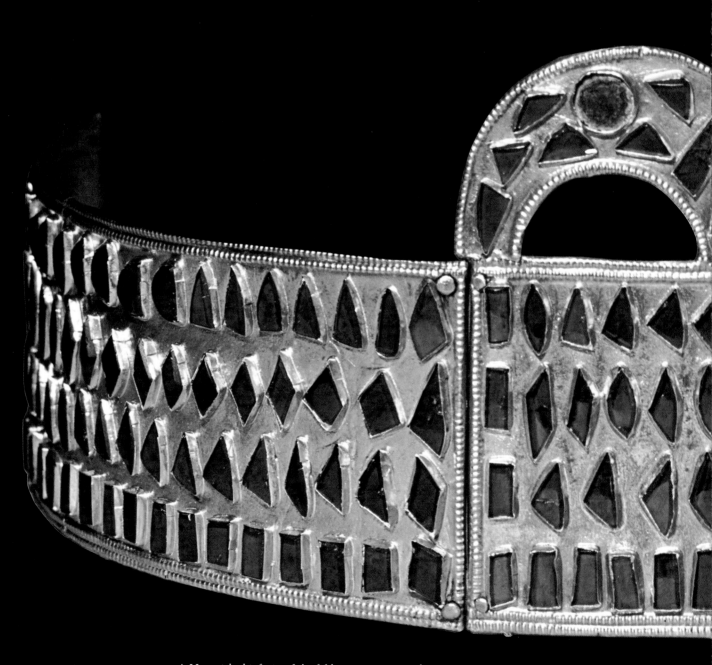

A Hunnish chieftain of the fifth century A.D. took this crown to his grave. The crown, made of gilded bronze and fitted with over 250 almandines, bears a stylized eagle—an emblem of supernatural power to the Huns.

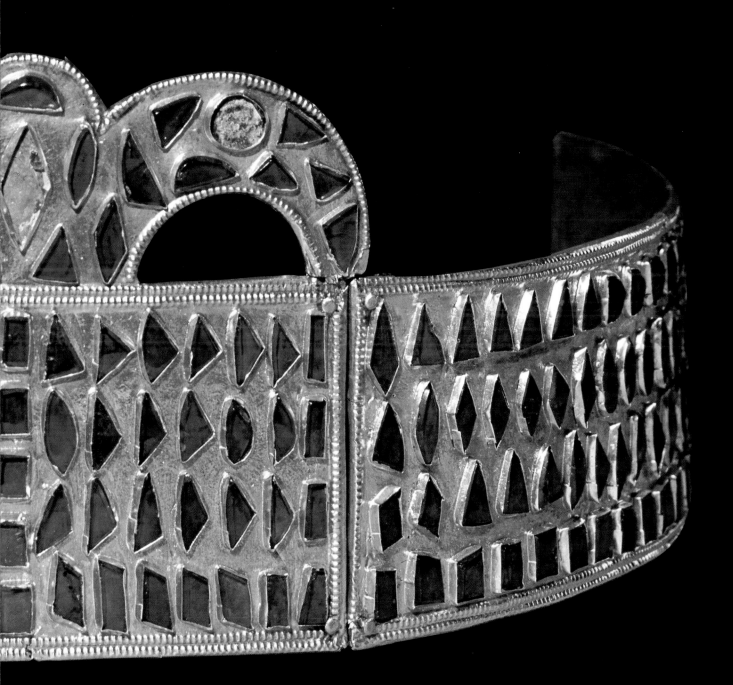

Visigothic war chiefs belted their tunics and fastened them with buckles such as these five from the early sixth century. Each gilt-bronze buckle consists of a looped catch and a rectangular plaque bearing embellishments indicating wealth and status. Artisans set the buckles with carnelians, almandines, metal bosses, and bits of colored glass and etched abstract designs into the gilded surfaces.

SEVENTH-CENTURY GERMANIC BROOCH

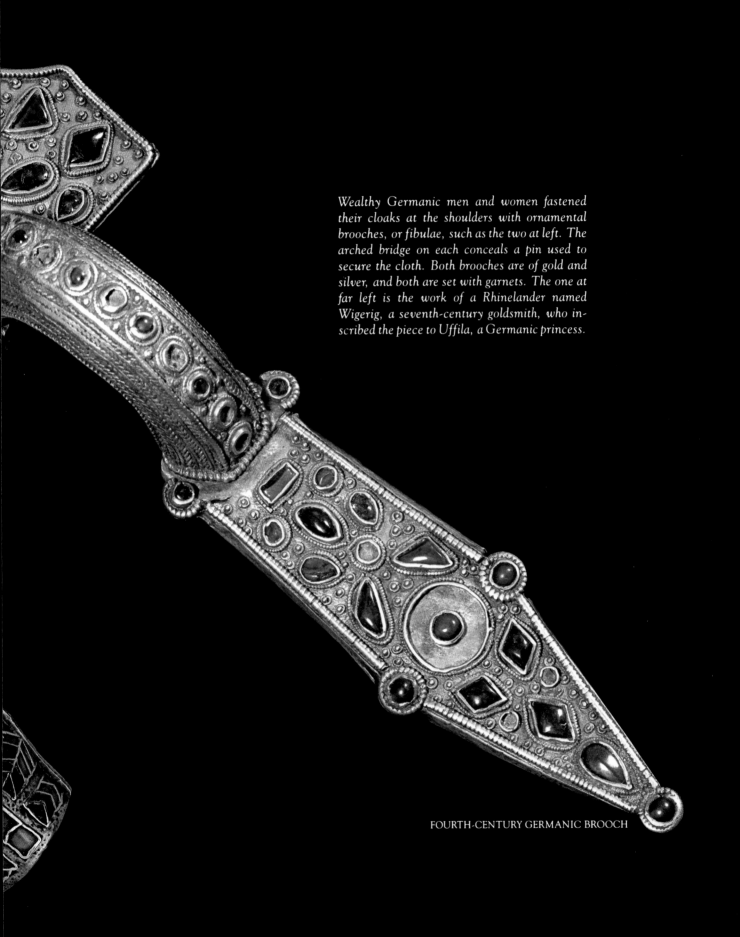

Wealthy Germanic men and women fastened their cloaks at the shoulders with ornamental brooches, or fibulae, such as the two at left. The arched bridge on each conceals a pin used to secure the cloth. Both brooches are of gold and silver, and both are set with garnets. The one at far left is the work of a Rhinelander named Wigerig, a seventh-century goldsmith, who inscribed the piece to Uffila, a Germanic princess.

FOURTH-CENTURY GERMANIC BROOCH

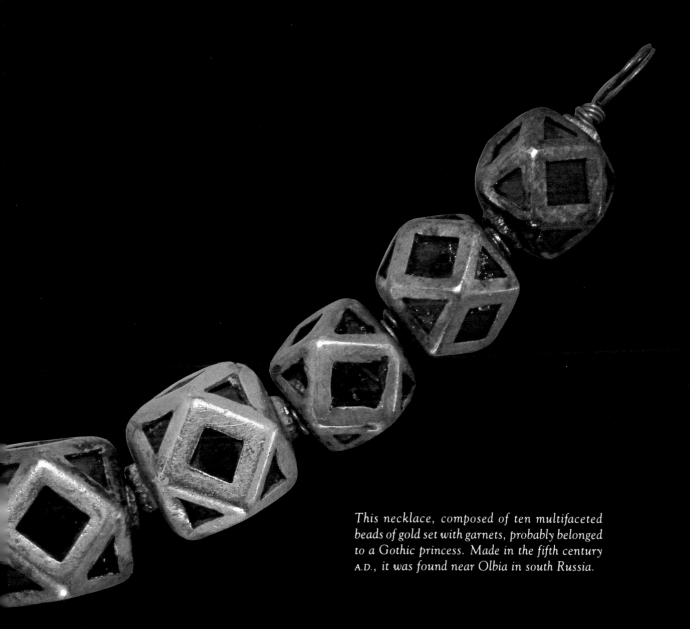

This necklace, composed of ten multifaceted beads of gold set with garnets, probably belonged to a Gothic princess. Made in the fifth century A.D., it was found near Olbia in south Russia.

This cross, made from strips of gold and set with domed gemstones, was a Visigothic king's gift to his church. Originally other gems hung from the arms of the cross, which was itself a pendant from a crown like the one opposite. The treasure is from a seventh-century royal hoard in Spain.

King Recceswinth gave this jewel-encrusted gold crown to his church in the Visigothic capital of Toledo in the seventh century, where it hung over the altar by its heart-shaped chains. Golden characters (in detail overleaf) and crystal and sapphire pendants dangle from the body of the crown.

OVERLEAF: The golden letters suspended from the crown above spell out the name of King Recceswinth. The wide band of gold, pierced with a delicate fern pattern, holds pearls and sapphires.

IV

FRANKS AND SAXONS

THE OUTSIDERS COME IN

In the city of Tournai in Belgium stands the church of Saint-Brice, a venerable building whose foundations go back to the eleventh century. Over three hundred years ago, in 1653, a tomb filled with treasure came to light along its north side. It held magnificent weapons and armor, a cloak gorgeously decorated with some three hundred gold bees, a massive gold signet ring, a fine gold bracelet, a gold buckle, a miniature bull's head in gold, a purse with one hundred gold coins, and a box with two hundred coins of silver. By the body rested the severed head of a horse, with all its harness. The head made it clear that the man buried here had been a barbarian, all the rest that he had been no ordinary barbarian.

An inscription on the ring gave the answer: he was Childeric, father of Clovis (the great ruler of the Franks), and hence the symbolic ancestor of the French monarchy. Napoleon himself was proud to use Childeric's bees to adorn his coronation robe when he was crowned emperor of France in 1804. Unfortunately little more than two of the bees and the sword and battle-ax remain of Chil-

A mounted warrior on a sixth-century-A.D. plaque epitomizes the resoluteness of the Franks, who along with the Anglo-Saxons outlasted all other Germanic tribes.

One of the greatest Anglo-Saxon rulers was Offa, whose name and likeness appear on a penny he introduced in 760. As king of Mercia (the Midlands), he unified much of England, and his coinage formed the basis of English currency for several centuries.

deric's riches. In 1831 robbers got into the chamber in Paris where the treasure was kept and made off with the best part of it.

The Franks were a federation of Germanic tribes that originally inhabited the lower reaches of the Rhine. Childeric and Clovis belonged to a cluster that the Romans called Salian Franks, "salty Franks," because they lived closest to the North Sea. In the third century A.D. the Salian Franks, together with other Frankish allies, pushed westward into what is now Belgium and then on into Gaul. Though Romans and Romanized Celts were all about them, they stubbornly kept to their ancestral ways. They still would ceremonially decapitate a corpse before burying it, and in the case of a great chieftain, such as Childeric, they also severed the head of his war-horse and put it in the grave. They went into battle naked to the waist or with only a light cloak, and their characteristic weapon was the *francisca,* a Frankish tomahawk. In 446 they seized Turnacum—Tournai, as it is called today—which for centuries had been a bustling Gallo-Roman town, and established their court there.

Childeric had his ups and downs before arriving at his sumptuous burial at Tournai. For a while his enemies managed to drive him into exile; the king of Thuringia (in what is now East Germany) graciously took him in—and was repaid by seeing his wife go off with their guest; Childeric was, she insisted, the wisest, strongest, and most beautiful man on earth. He made her his queen, and Clovis was the product of their romantic union.

Childeric died in 481, when his son was but fifteen. It did not take the boy long to show his quality as a leader, to become *magnus et pugnator egregius,* "a great and outstanding fighter," as France's famed medieval historian Gregory of Tours called him. Clovis earned this title by turning his unruly Frankish followers into a disciplined army. When marching his men through friendly territory, he did not allow them to do any damage whatsoever; during March of every year he personally inspected all weapons to make sure they were properly taken care of; and, after a successful battle, he had all booty collected in one place and impartially distributed. Once, when he deliberately bypassed Reims out of consideration for his friend Remigius, the bishop of Reims, an insubordinate Frankish unit descended on the town, sacked the churches, and carried off a load of sacred objects. Remigius begged Clovis to return one large, particularly beautiful vase. At the allocation of the spoils, which took place in nearby Soissons, Clovis requested the vase as his share. All agreed except one soldier; with a blow of his francisca the soldier smashed the piece, announcing, "You get only what falls to you by lot." At the annual review the following March, Clovis spotted the fellow in the ranks, went up to him, and, claiming his weapons were not in order, seized the soldier's ax and threw it on the ground. As the man bent to pick it up, Clovis sliced off his head with a stroke of his own ax saying, "Remember the vase at Soissons!"

Clovis was the first of the Franks to convert to orthodox Christianity: he and three thousand of his men were baptized at Reims in 496. This won him allies among the Christianized Gallo-Romans. These alliances, together with Clovis's rigid discipline, careful maintenance of equipment, and the absolutely equitable division of the profits of war made the Frankish army invincible. By the time the great leader died, in 511, he had secured for his people all of Gaul except a strip along the Mediterranean. The court was no longer off to the east in Tournai but in Paris, and there Clovis was buried on the spot where the Pantheon now stands. He had made Childeric's little kingdom into one almost as large as modern France.

———

Just east of the homeland of the salty Franks, between the Rhine and the Elbe, lived the west German tribes known as the Saxons and, a little to the north of them, in the neck of the Danish peninsula, those called the Angles. The salty Franks, despite their name, concentrated on the conquest of land; the Angles and Saxons turned to the sea. "Every rower you see in their crews," wrote a Roman living in Gaul in the fifth century "seems to be a pirate captain. It's because all of them...learn and teach the art of freebooting....They are an enemy more brutal than any other enemy...."

Another penny bears the profile of King Aethelred II, ruler of England from 978 to 1016. Called Aethelred the Unready, he was unable to stave off the waves of Viking invaders, who plundered the realm and dominated it for twenty-five years after his death.

TEXT CONTINUED ON PAGE 116

FRANKISH SPLENDOR

Childeric I, born about 436, was the first of the Frankish kings to achieve great eminence, in part by allying himself with the shrinking Roman Empire to defeat invading armies of Visigoths. Indeed Childeric probably saw himself as a worthy successor to the Roman rulers of Gaul and also looked to Rome in modeling some of his jewelry, which together with his weapons were buried with him in a wealthy tomb at Tournai in Belgium. Much of this regalia, unearthed in 1653, was later stolen. The recovered pieces, some of them shown here, combine Roman forms with a barbarian taste for brilliantly colored ornamentation.

Equally unstinting in the use of polychrome are the trappings of a sixth-century Frankish queen buried in the crypt of an abbey that stands outside Paris. The lady was probably Arnegunde, a consort to Chlothar I, sole king of the Franks from 558 to 561. At death the queen's body was embalmed and draped in luxurious garments—a linen shift, a silk tunic, a full-length red silk mantle—and then arrayed in jewels, including the pieces on pages 114 and 115. The rest of Arnegunde's tomb was comparatively simple; but her elaborate gold and garnet ornaments are exceptional among women's treasures of any barbarian aristocracy.

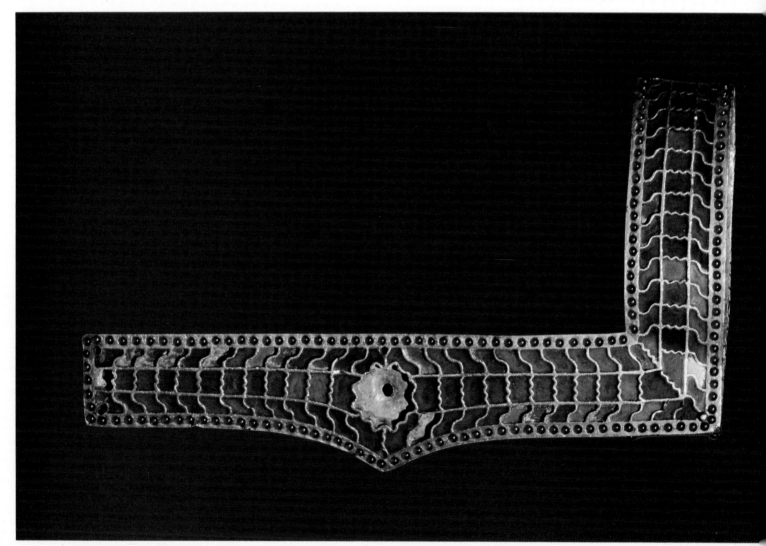

Two sword ornaments from Childeric's tomb are elegantly decorated in cloisonné with lustrous garnets set into narrow, wavy gold cells. The

A pair of fibulae, or tiny brooches, in the shape of bees have wings inlaid with almandine, a type of garnet. Some three hundred of these ornaments were sewn onto the brocaded cloak that was buried with King Childeric.

The figure of the king, his hair worn long in the style of Frankish royalty and a spear over his shoulder, is engraved on this gold signet ring, along with the name "Childerici Regis." The ring is a cast made before the original treasure was stolen.

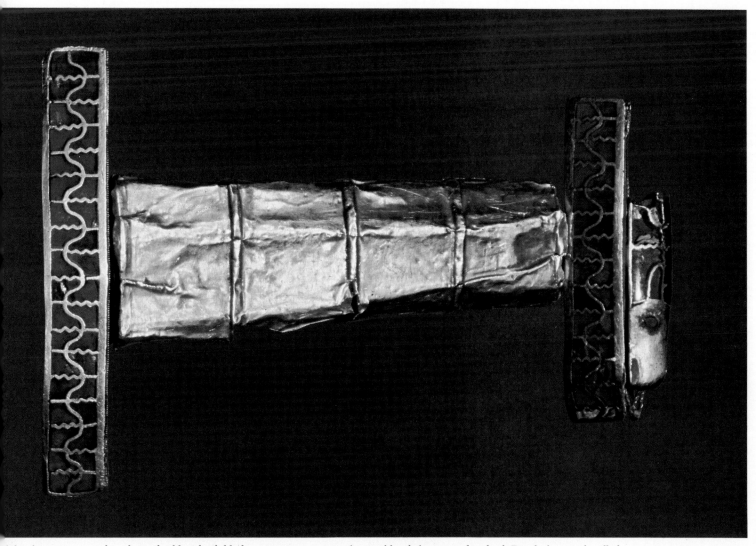

hilt above went with a long double-edged blade; opposite is part of a scabbard for a single-edged Frankish sword called a scramasax.

These gold brooches filled with garnets in intricate cloisonné closed Queen Arnegunde's mantle at the neck and waist. The design on each contains a cross within a cross, a sign that the queen was Christian.

For the two plates of a large belt buckle at right, a smith combined gold and silver and adorned the metals with filigree and with bosses along the edges to cap the rivets. Undoubtedly a man's buckle, it was a burial gift to Arnegunde.

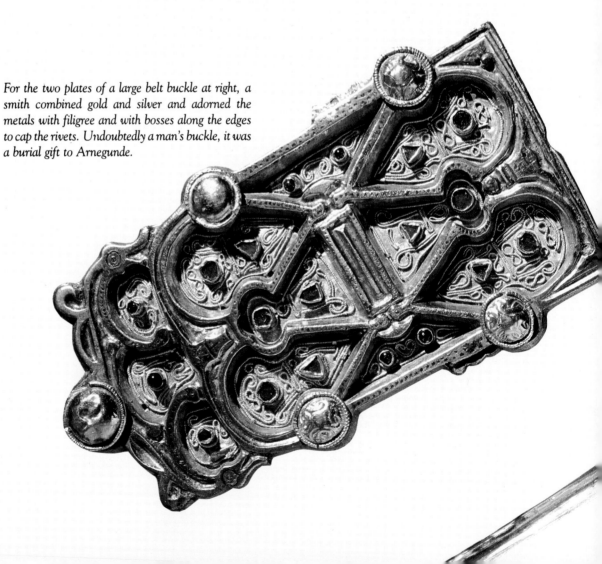

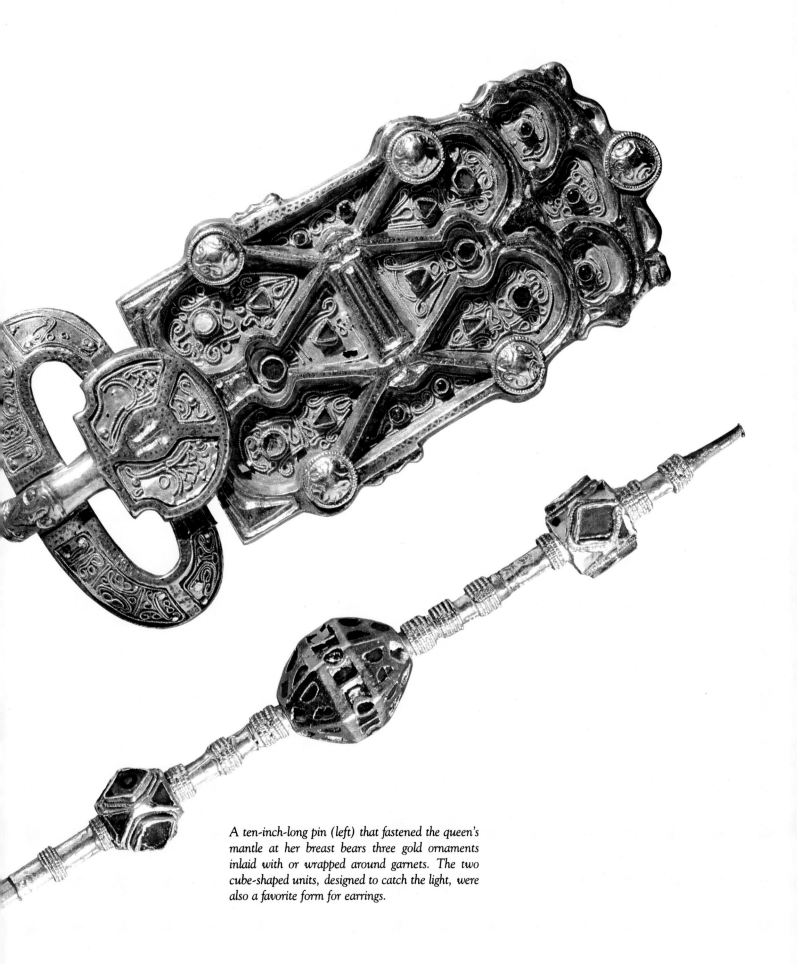

A ten-inch-long pin (left) that fastened the queen's mantle at her breast bears three gold ornaments inlaid with or wrapped around garnets. The two cube-shaped units, designed to catch the light, were also a favorite form for earrings.

TEXT CONTINUED FROM PAGE 111

The Angles and the Saxons had a free hand on the northern waters; the Franks, busy on land, left the seas to them. Sailing in high-prowed, long boats, powered by oar or sail, very much like those the Vikings were to use later, Anglo-Saxon raiders ranged along Holland and Belgium and even established permanent pockets of settlement on the French coast, near Boulogne and Bayeux. A favored target of their forays was the east coast of Britain. About 450 they ceased merely hitting and running; they hit and stayed. The Roman government, faced with the growing menace of the barbarian invasion back home, had recalled the legions from Britain in 410. It was up to the native Celtic population to expel the interlopers. They did their best, particularly under a chief named Arthur; legend later elevated him to be the gracious king who presided over a round table of ironclad knights, but he probably was a Celtic warlord at the head of an army as roughhewn and raggle-taggle as the enemy. The Angles and Saxons were too strong for him and the other defenders. By 600 they held most of England.

And by 600 their conversion to Christianity was under way. It all began—at least according to a story told by England's early historian the so-called Venerable Bede—when a young prelate in Rome saw a group of young, male Angles on the slave block in Rome. Struck by their fair skin and blond hair, he asked who they were. When they told him, "Anguli," he responded "Angeli Dei"—"Not Angles but Angels," so to speak—and vowed to convert the whole race. His chance came when he became Pope Gregory, later called "the Great." He sent a missionary, Augustine, who landed in 597 and converted the Saxon leaders in short order—perhaps too short order since the bonds of faith rather quickly became undone. King Raedwald of East Anglia, for example, when he returned home from his baptism, set up two altars: one for Christ, the other for sacrificing victims to devils.

The famed Anglo-Saxon epic *Beowulf* makes abundantly clear how primitive were the surroundings and the style of life of even the greatest Saxon lords in Raedwald's day. A chieftain's hall was little more than a vast wooden shed, with a hearth down the middle and

Defending his home, an archer (above right) delivers a rain of arrows against attackers brandishing spears and shields. This detail, carved in whalebone on the lid of a seventh-century chest, is from a Norse saga presumably well known to Anglo-Saxons.

holes in the roof to let the smoke get out; people sat on rude benches lining the walls. But the chieftains themselves were far more ornate: they glittered with jewelry, with gold buckles, and cloisonné brooches set with garnets. It was finery purchased with the rewards of warring and freebooting. In a hill south of the Forth River in Scotland a hoard of silver flagons and dishes has been found that some Saxon of this period no doubt buried for safekeeping. The treasures had come from Gaul and they must have been loot from some church or mansion. A good many of the pieces were roughly hacked in two; perhaps a pair of gangs had cooperated in the raid, and this was their way of dividing the swag.

But the most spectacular proof of Anglo-Saxon wealth is provided by a tomb that came to light only in 1939, a tomb that outshines all others in England. The Sutton Hoo burial, named for the private estate where it was discovered, was in an Anglo-Saxon cemetery hard by a tidal estuary in East Anglia. It was a boat burial: the grave was an actual boat dragged up on land. The grave goods were deposited in it, and it was then covered over by a mound. The wood has totally vanished, destroyed by the action of the soil, but it left a stain on the sand and from this as well as from the bolts and rivets, which were all embedded in the soil in their original place, the craft can be reconstructed. It was eighty-nine feet long, a seagoing vessel with oars but no sail. And in it was a fortune in silver and gold, jewels and objects clearly pagan in origin, some of them imports from eastern Europe or the Near East, others bearing the Christian cross as decoration.

The tomb has justly been compared with Childeric's at Tournai. Childeric was king of the Franks; what king of East Anglia was buried at Sutton Hoo? The mystery may never be solved because there is no corpse at Sutton Hoo. Some authorities argue that there had been one but, like the wood, it was destroyed by the soil. Others claim that there never had been one, that Sutton Hoo was not an actual grave but a cenotaph—a memorial monument. That, of course, only leads to the questions: whose cenotaph and why a cenotaph? The clues are contradictory. Only a pagan would be given a boat

King Edmund, a Christian Anglo-Saxon, is seized by Viking raiders during an attack on England in 870. This scene from an eleventh-century English history illustrates one of the many clashes that occurred between Vikings and Anglo-Saxons.

burial—yet why would a pagan have bowls adorned with the cross in his grave? The coins were all collected about 625—though they could have been put in the boat any time later. But why so few? The total represents only a modest amount of money. And why so carefully picked? There are no duplications; each is of a different type and from a different mint.

The names of the kings of seventh-century East Anglia are all known, and two in the list are at present the front-running candidates. If Sutton Hoo is a cenotaph, then it could have been for King Sigebert, who died in 635 or 636. He had become a monk, so his remains would have gone into the monastery cemetery. The boat burial would have been staged to satisfy the tastes of his pagan subjects. If it was an actual grave, then it could have been for King Raedwald, who was converted to Christianity but still worshiped pagan gods, a circumstance which would explain the mix of pagan and Christian elements. He died in 624 or 625, precisely the date the coins point to.

What of the coins? As it happens this ship would certainly have needed a crew of forty oarsmen. Could not the forty coins be their pay for rowing the vessel to its destination in the afterlife? The two ingots, of higher value than the coins, might have been the pay of the steersmen. Whether cenotaph or tomb, the Sutton Hoo ship reveals that the Anglo-Saxon lords of the seventh century, rude barbarians though they were in so many ways, possessed treasures of great value and superb craftsmanship.

From the seventh century on, the contours of roughhewn Anglo-Saxons began rapidly to soften. The chieftain commemorated at Sutton Hoo still followed pagan ways; by the end of the seventh century, Christianity had triumphed throughout the land. By the end of the ninth, King Alfred the Great, having taught himself Latin, was turning out English translations of Latin works on history, theology, and philosophy. He set up a court school staffed by imported scholars of repute and issued orders that all young freemen who had the means must learn to read English. Anglo-Saxon barbarianism had vanished. The outsiders had become insiders.

A KING'S TROVE
AT SUTTON HOO

The richest of all known Anglo-Saxon tombs held these two shield ornaments made of gilt bronze and garnets, which represent the head (left) and talon of a fierce bird.

Some time in the first half of the seventh century, an Anglo-Saxon burial party hauled a huge open seagoing boat, some ninety feet long, from an estuary on the northeast English coast to a nearby heath, at a site now known as Sutton Hoo. Their purpose was to honor a deceased chieftain, in all likelihood a pagan king of East Anglia, and into the vessel they put the dead man's weapons and armor, a profusion of jewels, and other splendid trophies. Distributing the riches amidships they then made a barrow and sealed the ship under a great mound of earth.

Probably this was not an actual tomb but a cenotaph—a monument to a beloved leader whose body was lost in battle. For when at last uncovered in 1939, the Sutton Hoo ship burial held no trace of human remains. Its cargo is nevertheless incomparably rich, and it also reflects far-ranging foreign contacts: a helmet (opposite) which is Swedish in style; Frankish gold coins; a bronze hanging bowl, like that on pages 130–131, of Celtic origin; Germanic animal motifs; and the ritual of ship burial itself, very likely derived from pagan Viking rites.

However, the most magnificent objects interred at Sutton Hoo are pieces of cloisonné jewelry fashioned by Anglo-Saxon goldsmiths, many of them probably by a single master. Like the beautiful clasps on pages 126 and 127, most are made of gold superbly enhanced with garnets and colored glass; all told, more than four thousand of the deep red stones were cut and fitted into individual gold compartments. Whoever the dead noble of Sutton Hoo was, he clearly commanded the very finest in materials and craftsmanship that his age had to offer.

Eyebrows inlaid with silver wires, and a gilded nose and mouth, make up the features of an imposing helmet (opposite) reconstructed from fragments in the Sutton Hoo ship. An iron crest runs from front to back, beginning in animal heads with garnet eyes.

A bronze stag and ring crown a scepter, in detail above, made of fine-grained stone. Below the ornament gazes one of four solemn faces carved around the staff, which is a whetstone. Emblem of the king's office, the scepter has a support so that it could rest on his knee.

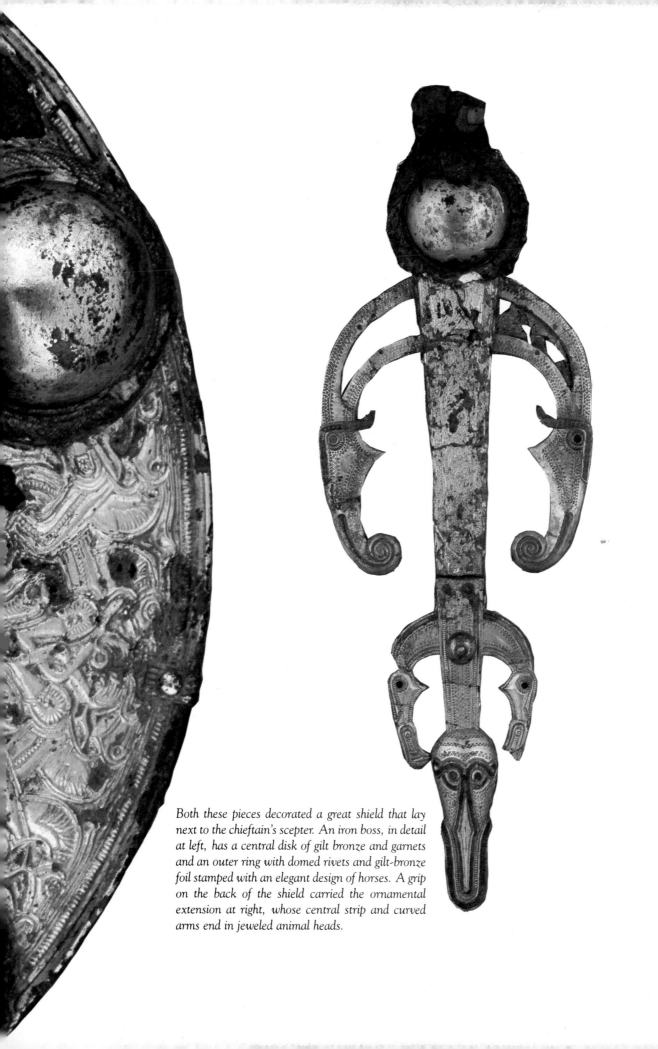

Both these pieces decorated a great shield that lay next to the chieftain's scepter. An iron boss, in detail at left, has a central disk of gilt bronze and garnets and an outer ring with domed rivets and gilt-bronze foil stamped with an elegant design of horses. A grip on the back of the shield carried the ornamental extension at right, whose central strip and curved arms end in jeweled animal heads.

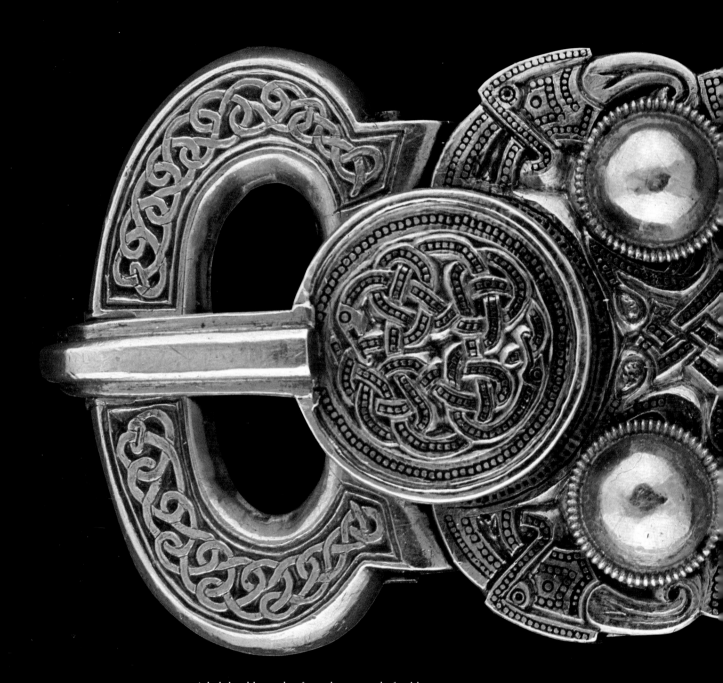

A belt buckle made of nearly a pound of gold was probably the chieftain's most important piece of jewelry. In its center, and on the circular plate at left supporting the buckle tongue, the artisan incised a wonderful maze of lines and dots that represent entwined snakes.

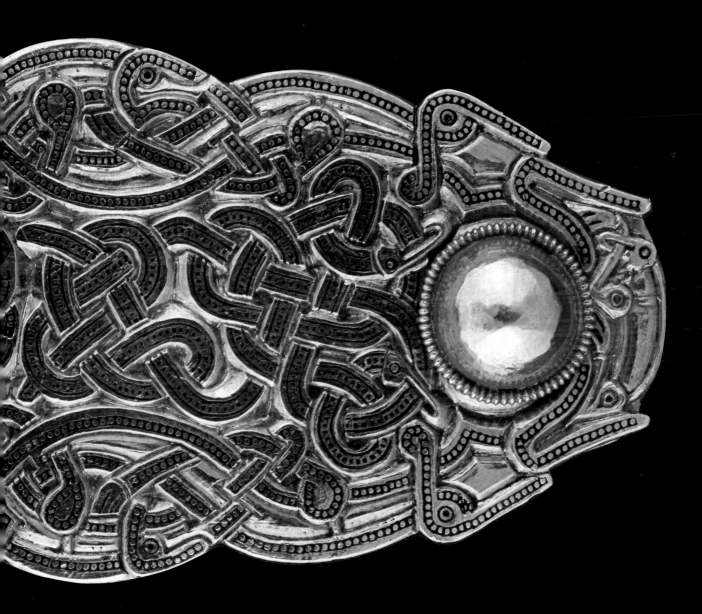

This gold shoulder clasp, consisting of two panels connected by a pin, presumably held a heavy garment or cuirass in place. It may mimic the shoulder fittings of Roman parade armor. The workmanship is spectacular, with cloisonné cells in a minute step pattern framed by interlacing lines, all inlaid with garnets and red glass. Garnets, glass, and gold filigree form animal motifs at the end of each panel, and the gold pin also ends in an animal head encrusted with filigree.

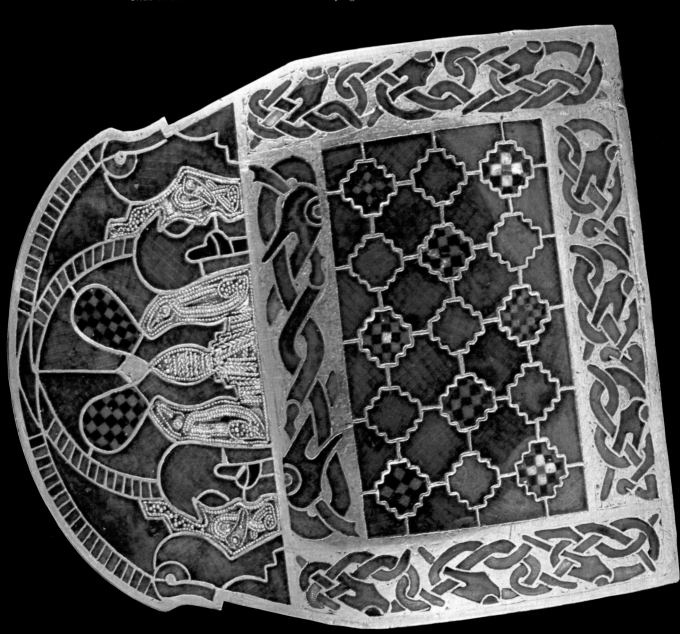

This hexagonal plaque, just over an inch high, adorned the lid of a purse that contained gold coins and blanks. Its painstaking cloisonné work—gold cells set with garnets—displays the intricacy and sumptuousness of a fine tapestry.

On a second plaque from the same purse lid, a bird of prey with hooked beak descends on a duck. The tail feathers and wings of both animals are cloisonné, while the eyes are round garnets containing tiny engraved circles filled with blue glass.

This bronze vessel with rings on the rim and ornamental plates (detail pages 132–133) along the
sides was designed to be hung. But the function
of such bowls—prestige items in many Saxon
graves—is a mystery. This one appears to be the
work of Celts, who perhaps used it in religious
rituals until pagan Saxons seized it as loot.

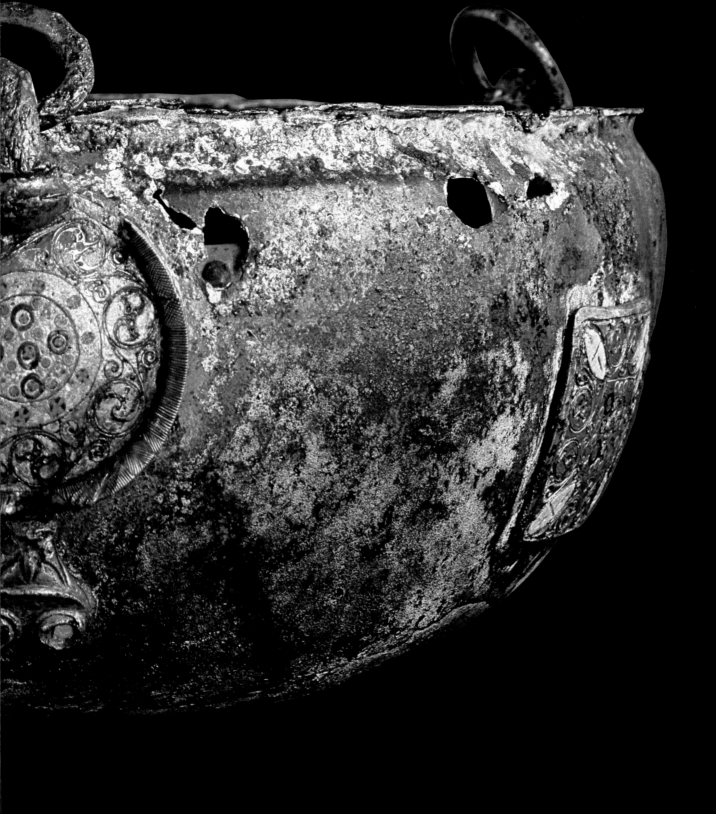

A square, bronze border surrounds an intricately embellished escutcheon of red enamel in this detail from the hanging bowl on the preceding pages. Small plaques of gilded bronze point from each corner, with fine bronze scrollwork set between them. At the center, also enclosed in a square, are inlays of colored glass shaped into minute rosettes and checkerboards.

V

THE VIKING MARAUDERS

WARRIORS OF THE LONGBOATS

I n the summer of 921, a secretary of the caliph of Baghdad, Ibn
Fadlan, went on a mission to the king of the Bulgars, a Slavic
people living along the middle Volga in what is now the Soviet
Union. Along his way he passed a community of Rus—Viking
traders from Sweden—who had camped along the river to sell off
their load of slaves. Ibn Fadlan, an inquisitive observer and a vivid
writer, decided to record what he saw. One can imagine the fas-
tidious Arab's nose wrinkling in disgust at Viking ways.

They are the filthiest people under god. They never wash off excrement or
urine; they do not wash after sexual relations; they do not wash their hands
after meals. They are like wild donkeys.
When they arrive from their country they anchor their boats on the Atul
[the Volga], which is a mighty river, and build along its banks large wooden
houses. In each one of these, ten and twenty people, more or less, live
together. Each has a bed on which he rests. With them are beautiful young
female slaves intended for the slave merchants. Each of the men will have
sexual relations with his slave with his companions looking on. Sometimes

*Scandinavian warriors prepare for battle, one so eager that he bites his shield. These
marauders are twelfth-century chessmen exquisitely carved from walrus tusk.*

Sail unfurled, two Vikings on this detail of an early grave marker from Gotland set out on the voyage to paradise, Valhalla. There under the eye of the chief god, Odin, fallen warriors lived on forever to fight by day, and by night to feast and drink.

whole bunches of them unite in this manner, one in front of the other. If a slave merchant enters to buy a young slave from one of them and finds the master in the midst of having relations with her, the master does not withdraw from her before having satisfied his needs.

Every day they must wash their face and head, and they do it in the dirtiest and filthiest way possible. Every morning the young serving girl arrives carrying a large bowl full of water. She puts it before her master, and he washes his hands and his face as well as his hair. He washes and combs out his hair into the basin, and then blows his nose and spits and does every other possible filthy act into this water. When he has finished what he has to do, the servant girl carries the bowl to the man next to him, and this one does just as his companion had done. She continues to pass the bowl from one to the other till it has made the circle of all who live in the house.

The Rus buried their dead in flamboyant Viking style. Ibn Fadlan had the great good luck to pass through when preparations were under way for the funeral of a chieftain. It was a boat burial but, unlike the burial at Sutton Hoo, this Viking burial ended with cremation of the boat, the body, and all. What is more, a key element was the ritual murder of a slave girl to accompany her lord to the afterlife. She was a volunteer, and during the period of time it took to get ready for the funeral she lived in splendor. Says Ibn Fadlan, "She is entrusted to two other young female slaves who watch over her and are with her wherever she goes, to the point of at times washing her feet with their own hands." When the fatal day arrived, she paid a visit to the various Rus notables and had sexual relations with each. Each instructed her, "Tell your master that I did this only out of love for him."

The men pulled the boat for the burial up on the bank of the river, propped it up with stakes, and stacked firewood underneath. On it they set up a tent with a bed inside, covered with a brocaded spread and brocaded cushions, for the corpses of the chief and the girl. An old woman, who was called the Angel of Death, directed her movements. At the appropriate moment:

the old woman seized her by the head and bade her go into the tent and entered along with her. Then the men set about beating with their clubs on their shields so that no one would hear the sound of her cries and other slave girls would not be frightened and would not try to escape death with their masters. Next six men entered the tent and had relations with the young girl. Next they laid her down beside her master. Two seized her feet, two others her hands. The old woman called the Angel of Death came up, put a cord about her neck so that the two ends were apart and gave it to the two men to pull. Then she went up to the girl, holding a dagger with a wide blade, and kept plunging it between the ribs and pulling it out while the two men strangled with the cord until the girl was dead.

The last act was to set fire to this grisly bier. "The fire swept over the wood, then the boat, then the tent, the corpse, the girl and all that was on the boat."

These Swedish Vikings, whose ways Ibn Fadlan describes so graphically, together with their Danish and Norwegian counterparts, were in a sense historical throwbacks. They were still rough primitives at a time when the Celts, the Goths, the Saxons, and the Franks had already joined the ranks of the civilized. And just as these had once pounced on and plundered the enticing treasures of the Romans, so now the Vikings pounced on and plundered the treasures of the Slavs in Russia, of the Frankish empire in Europe, of the Anglo-Saxons, and of the Irish. They descended upon Italy, North Africa, and the Byzantine empire, burning, looting, and enslaving, but also at times behaving as peaceable merchants. Their longboats would take them anywhere; as long as the seas were open to them, no land was safe from them.

"Came three ships of Northmen. . . . And then the reve sheriff rode to the place, and would have driven them to the king's residence, because he knew not who they were: and they slew him. These were the first ships of Danishmen which sought the land of the English nation." So wrote the compiler of the *Anglo-Saxon Chronicle* under the date 787. Six years later, as the entry for 793 records, "the ravaging of heathen men lamentably destroyed God's church at Lindisfarne through rapine and slaughter." Lindisfarne was an island

The mythical hero Sigurd leaps out of a trench and plunges his sword into the vulnerable belly of the dragon Fáfnir in this carving on a wooden portal of a Norwegian church. The legend of Sigurd, or Siegfried, replete with bloodletting and treachery, was known throughout the Viking world.

off the coast of England near its border with Scotland and the site of a venerable monastic community. When the "heathen men"—either Danes or Norwegians—quit the place, most of the monks had been murdered or carried off for sale and the buildings looted and burned. These were the first recorded acts of violence committed by the Vikings in the west.

Ibn Fadlan's Rus, coming from Sweden, whose coastline faces east, focused upon that direction. The Vikings of Denmark and Norway, geographically oriented the opposite way, concentrated on the west. For four hundred years after the attack upon Lindisfarne, their bands descended upon western Europe. A good part of that time, until roughly A.D. 1000, the marauders were heathen, and so monasteries, convents, and churches were not only fair game but, being the richest institutions around, the preferred game. What made the Vikings' attacks so hard to parry was not their invincibility in battle. Indeed their favored weapon, the battle-ax, had long been abandoned by less primitive peoples, their swords were inferior to those the Franks used, and they never got the hang of besieging a fortification. But on the sea they were invincible, thanks to their superb ships and skilled seamanship.

The Viking longship, lean and efficient, with its high prow curving into the wind, was one of the swiftest fighting galleys ever devised. Built of overlapping oak staves, a ship of medium size would be about eighty feet long but shallow—less than six feet from the oarlock to the bottom of the keel—so that it fairly flew over the water. It carried as rudder a single steering oar on the starboard side. Amidships rose a mast with a single square sail—the unmistakable red and white spread of canvas that brought instant terror to any shore dweller who caught sight of it. Aboard such a vessel was a crew of fifty or more rowers and warriors. A fleet of these ships, roped together, formed an impregnable seagoing battle line, which few medieval sea captains cared to attack. These greyhounds of the sea were the Vikings' prime weapon. They assured so total a command of the water that no force ever successfully engaged the Vikings there. They were able at will to make swift and sudden onslaughts and, if

The Normans inherited the ship craft of their Viking ancestors, which included the ability to measure the sweep of a hull by eye. Here in a detail from the Bayeux Tapestry—the famous embroidery that records the events of 1066—Normans construct a fleet for their coming invasion of England.

pressed, they were able to beat hasty and safe retreats.

The Rus were oriented toward eastern Europe. Moreover, they were as much interested in trade as in plunder. Finding their best customers in the rich caliphate of Baghdad, they penetrated deeper and deeper into Russia to reduce the number of middlemen required to pass along their goods to the Near East and to acquire directly the luxury goods they themselves wanted—silks, glass, silver, and bronze. The Rus sold furs and slaves; the first came from the forests of their homeland, the second from the Slavic populations through which they passed (thereby helping to make "Slav" the origin of our word "slave").

From the end of the eighth century on, their ships nosed past the coasts of Finland, up the Baltic rivers in the east Russian plain, and down the Volga. As time went on many of the Rus settled in Russia. A certain Rurik built up a powerful Viking state based at Novgorod, some 125 miles south of Leningrad. In 880 Rurik's successor Oleg captured Kiev and established his rule over the whole of the trade route from the Gulf of Finland to the Black Sea. Novgorod, Kiev, Rostov, Smolensk, and others, all commercial centers that the Rus either founded or set in motion, played a significant part in the development whereby the country's miscellaneous Slavic tribes eventually merged into a political whole. They became the "Russian" state—the very name points to the importance of the Viking contribution.

The Danish Vikings, as was natural, turned westward. Their favored targets were France and England, although more adventurous spirits went far beyond, even penetrating the Mediterranean to attack Seville, as well as Cadiz. Once a pack wintered in southern France and the next spring, nicely refreshed, sailed on to Italy where they sacked Pisa. Their victims were unable to stop the Vikings by force of arms, and in desperation they turned to other measures. Every now and then a local ruler tried hiring a compliant group of Vikings to help him fight off their brothers. Unfortunately they had a nasty tendency to go off on their own. In 862 the Vikings that the count of Anjou had hired to fight other Vikings went on to burn an

TEXT CONTINUED ON PAGE 146

A QUEEN SAILS TO THE AFTERLIFE

Ferocious kings, not queens, dominate Viking history, but one woman ranks with any of them in her taste for vengeance: Asa, daughter of a minor Viking aristocrat. Gudrod the Magnificent, ruler of a small Norwegian kingdom, kidnapped Asa and forced her to marry him. She bore him a son, but a year after the birth her hatred was unabated, and she ordered a servant to spear Gudrod to death as he lay in a drunken stupor. Then she ruled alone.

When she died in about 850, Asa's followers placed her body aboard an oaken longship along with that of a maidservant, whom the Vikings had probably killed ritualistically for the occasion. They furnished the ship with everything that a queen would need in the afterlife and buried the vessel near Oseberg.

Before the ship was unearthed in 1904, robbers had looted the gold and gems that presumably had been aboard. But the items that remain, including four sleds and a wagon, testify to the high craft of those who made them and to the Viking passion for travel, by whatever conveyance. The lines of the ship itself bear witness to the shipwright's skill that opened up the known and the unknown world to a people previously isolated by the sea.

Mysterious beasts with pear-shaped limbs grasp each other by foot and claw in a carved pattern repeated along the ship's stem and stern. Such creatures are a common motif in Scandinavian art, but what they symbolize is still a mystery.

The stern and prow of the Oseberg ship soar sixteen feet above deck. At seventy-one feet it is as long as a warship, but its light build and unprotected oar holes (fifteen to a side) mark it as a state barge.

A bug-eyed monster roars from the top of a post that was found in Queen Asa's funeral trove. At sea such posts were lashed to the prow to ward off evil spirits and to assure good luck during battle.

The carved wooden cart at left, buried inside Queen Asa's ship, is the only complete example that has survived of the Viking wheelwright's craft. Carvings illustrating myths and legends cover the cart's curved body. The fierce face above is one of four that snarl from each end of the pair of curved staves supporting the tublike carriage, which held cargo, not passengers. The beards, however, were practical. They probably served as convenient handles for wresting the cart out of mudholes.

This is one of three decoratively carved, horse-drawn sleds on the Oseberg ship, all designed for traveling by land. A fourth sled, less ornate, was on board, presumably as a baggage cart. On each corner is a ferocious animal head.

TEXT CONTINUED FROM PAGE 139

abbey and then to hold up the city of Poitiers for ransom.

Eventually the king of France decided that since it was impossible to lick them, he would join them. In 911 Charles the Simple ennobled the leader of a powerful band of Danes. Hrolfr—or Rollo, to give him his more pronounceable name—had laid hold of Normandy, and Charles made him the first duke of Normandy, the acknowledged ruler of the lands he actually held. For the king it turned out to be an astute move. In exchange Rollo swore allegiance to the crown and helped France fend off other Vikings. Although his men hardly became well-behaved citizens overnight, time and intermarriage with local women gradually changed them from Norsemen to Normans. A century later Rollo's descendant William pounced on England and made it his own.

But the most common practice in tenth-century Christendom was to buy the Vikings off. This swiftly degenerated into blackmail, for the Danes insisted on regular payments—the notorious Danegeld, the Viking age version of protection money, which was the gold handed over to the Danes to buy off their attacks. The amount of treasure, particularly silver, that the Vikings pocketed this way was astronomical. In 994 the Norwegians under the famous leader Olaf Tryggvesson and the Danes under the equally famous Sven Forkbeard joined forces for a descent upon England. The English king paid them sixteen thousand pounds of silver to go away. The record amount of Danegeld was achieved by Sven's son Knud (also known as Canute), who had succeeded in bringing all of England under his rule; he levied 10,500 pounds on London alone and 72,000 on the rest of the country. He kept some of the wealth for himself and divided the rest among his retainers.

The Norwegian Vikings concentrated on the northern part of Britain and on Ireland. Although all the Vikings were expert seamen, the Norwegians, coming from a home whose coast was lined with excellent harbors facing the ocean, became the most skilled and daring. In the course of time they sent their galleys far beyond the shores of Ireland, over the open water. By 800 Viking seafarers had found their way to the Faroe Islands, and a century later

Olaf Tryggvesson, tenth-century king of Norway, delivers a deathblow to a sea ogress, one of many that lurked beneath the sea, surfacing only to capsize Viking vessels. This is a detail from an illustrated Icelandic saga about Olaf's exploits.

they were established in Iceland. In 986 the intrepid Eric the Red led a group of colonists to the coast of Greenland. And then, just about 1000, Eric's son Leif launched the expedition that has made him the best known of all the Vikings: he sailed with a party of thirty-five from Greenland across the north Atlantic. According to the Icelandic saga that tells of his feat, he landed in a place where there was abundant timber, the rivers and sea teemed with the biggest salmon they had ever seen, the grass was green almost all year round, and—most surprising of all to him—there were vines bearing grapes; this was so surprising that he called the place Wineland, or, to give it the form commonly used today, Vinland.

Leif's story is not found in archival documents or chronicles but in poems chanted by Icelandic bards centuries after his lifetime. There have always been skeptics who thought there was more bardic license in the poems than fact. But recent archaeological findings at a spot called L'Anse aux Meadows in the northernmost tip of Newfoundland have put it beyond doubt. The excavators came upon indisputable proof of the existence of a colony of Norsemen there just about A.D. 1000; they may even have been Leif's very band or descendants of them. They set up house and boat sheds, the remains of which have come to light along with a few other objects.

There is no question that the Norwegians had the boats for such a voyage. In the last century two well-preserved boat burials were discovered in Norway, at Gokstad and at Oseberg. In the Gokstad ship, a graceful but sturdy galley of oak built to take the boisterous northern seas, a Viking chieftain had been laid to rest in about 900. Around him was the gear he would need in his afterlife: kettles, plates, cups, candlesticks, and so on, but not his jewelry or the money to pay his rowers or anything precious; grave robbers had made off with all that centuries earlier. The Oseberg burial is from about half a century before the Gokstad. The ship, also of oak, is of lighter construction, intended for coastal work; it is a particularly elegant craft, decorated with fine carving. It held the bodies of two women, one young and one old; the older was a noblewoman and perhaps Queen Asa, grandmother of Norway's famous King Harald

Harald Bluetooth, the king who unified the Danes, was baptized a Christian about 960 by a monk named Poppo. This twelfth-century gold relief commemorates the event. On his own orders Harald was buried in one of the country's first cathedrals—but he also ordered himself a Viking burial, probably in case he wanted to visit his ancestors after death.

Fairhair. The grave goods in her tomb included a beautifully carved carriage and sledges and furniture, as well as the customary kitchen equipment, but of the treasure that must have been there, the jewelry and silver plate, there was hardly a trace; grave robbers had done their usual efficient job.

Around the middle of the tenth century, Denmark's hard-fighting King Harald Bluetooth converted to Christianity, and one of the achievements that he proudly reported on a stone column he erected was that he had made his kingdom Christian. It took the Norwegians longer; Olaf Tryggvesson had been baptized during a foray into England; in 995 he became king of Norway, and he and his successors accomplished the conversion of his people. The Swedes were laggards. In the eleventh century their kings were Christian, but the country at large did not follow until as late as 1100. This spelled the end, once and for all, of treasure-laden boat graves.

Up to the beginning of the Christian Era, the trackless expanses of Europe beyond the rim of Greco-Roman civilization were inhabited by barbarian tribes. These were drawn irresistibly by the glitter of what Greco-Roman civilization had to offer—its treasures and its pleasures. The Scythians managed to stand somewhat aloof and persuaded the Greeks to bring the treasures to them. The Celts, after some gallant dashes across the rim, had a sea of Greeks and Romans flood over them; only in Ireland and later in Brittany did they avoid being Romanized. Certain powerful Germanic tribes, like the Goths and Vandals, dived into the sea themselves, and became submerged in the waters of civilization as had the Celts.

A good two centuries after Europe had absorbed so many of these barbarians—no longer outsiders—it was suddenly buffeted by yet another wave out of Scandinavia and in a sense held for ransom by them. Yet even the Vikings were eventually absorbed. In their homeland they continued to be Danes and Nowegians and Swedes. But they ceased being outsiders. They ceased burying their treasure in graves and began displaying it in churches.

SEAFARERS'
HOARDS

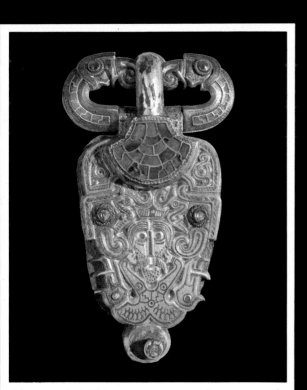

A moustached Norseman stares out from a seventh-century bronze buckle inlaid with silver. The design includes birds and animal heads, inset garnets, and glass beads.

Viking artisans who worked in gold, silver, bronze, and precious stones left a legacy that speaks not only of their own extraordinary skills but also of the almost endearing vanity of their patrons. Viking men as well as women loved to festoon themselves with elaborate accessories. Much of the art produced by Viking metalsmiths and jewelers was functional, such as the wind vane at left. Other creations were auxiliary to the waging of war, such as the sword and riding tack on the following pages. But beyond that they produced a dazzling array of belt buckles and brooches, as well as necklaces and pendants.

Whatever the function of each piece, stylized animal motifs always dominate the designs, which grew incredibly complex as the centuries passed. Tresses of vegetation wind around snakes and sea monsters so that the human figures are often difficult to find amid the convoluted, often frenzied patterns wherein they cavort, leer, and sometimes kill one another.

In Viking art lies convincing evidence of Viking ferocity—and of their belief in demons, magic, and dark gods. Yet no people ever took more pleasure in finesse and delicacy when it came to creating a belt buckle or sword hilt. And few people ranged wider in their quest for treasure, which they enjoyed in life and confidently expected to possess after death.

A majestic creature (above), sometimes known as the "Great Beast," stands guard at the tip of a gilt-bronze wind vane, made in Norway early in the eleventh century. Other animals and birds cavort amid vegetation on the engraved body of the vane. The holes were for pendants or ribbons.

Geometric patterns, a bird, a serpent, and crosses (the latter a pre-Christian design) decorate this silver-encrusted sword hilt. It was found at Hedeby, Denmark, a major Viking trading center and a rich site for buried Viking hoards.

For weapons the Vikings prized Frankish iron most highly, but whatever the provenience, a Viking sword was a weapon of swift efficiency. The example above from the tenth century, found in Steinsvik, Norway, bears bronze ornaments on pommel and guard.

Gold wire entwines the handle of this tenth-century sword (right), unearthed in Sweden. The pommel and guard are both decorated in silver. The blade, like the others on these pages, was corroded during a burial that lasted some ten centuries.

VIKING HARNESS BOW OR HORSE COLLAR

The arc of gilt bronzework mounted on wood, above, was an ordinary piece of riding gear that lay across a horse's mane with reins threaded through it. Yet the animal head, opposite, from the end of the collar, is more supernatural than functional. Birds and animals cast in low relief decorate its snout, and scaly animals in flight form the wrinkles on its cheeks and brow. Silver plate adds glitter to its teeth, eyebrows, and lips. All this befit a bug-eyed, bat-eared dragon, an image of evil.

OVERLEAF: In this second detail of the collar, two dragons sink their fangs into the central openwork design, which is composed of yet another pair of monsters—this time with interlaced bodies, which ingeniously complete the loops for the reins. So elaborate a piece may have belonged to a great chieftain, who used it as a harness part for his horse. The piece, workaday but extravagant, may represent the zenith of the Viking craftsman's skill in combining the decorative with the practical.

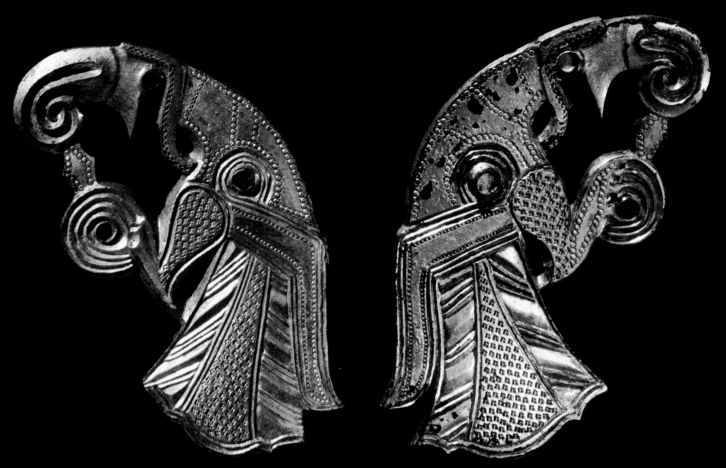

These stylized ravens, cast of bronze and gilded,
once decorated the harness or sword hilt of a
distinguished Viking horseman. The lustrous
raven symbolized the Viking cult of Odin.

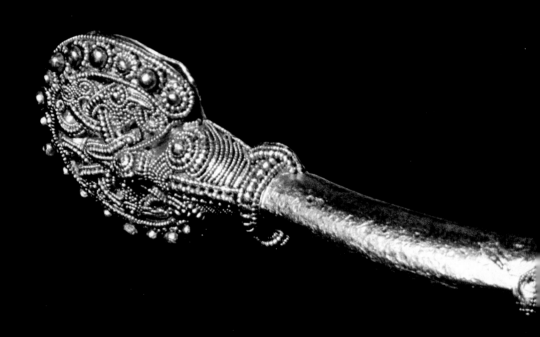

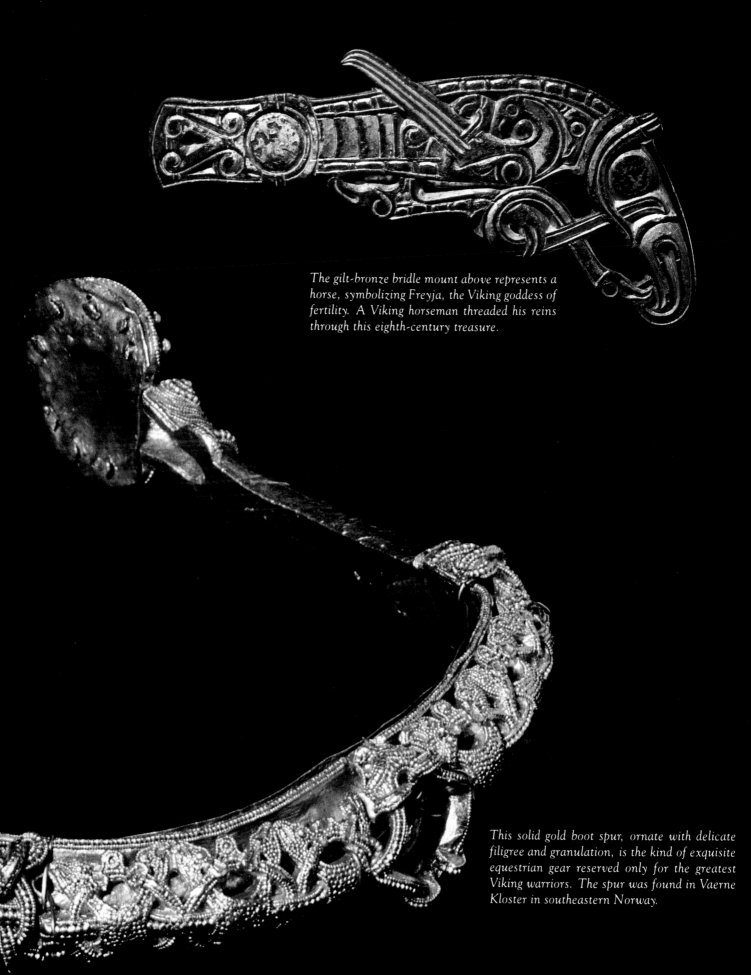

The gilt-bronze bridle mount above represents a horse, symbolizing Freyja, the Viking goddess of fertility. A Viking horseman threaded his reins through this eighth-century treasure.

This solid gold boot spur, ornate with delicate filigree and granulation, is the kind of exquisite equestrian gear reserved only for the greatest Viking warriors. The spur was found in Vaerne Kloster in southeastern Norway.

This gold collar, in detail overleaf, belonged to a sixth-century Viking king.

A crude rendition of a Roman emperor on horseback occupies the center of the gold pendant opposite, an amulet that a mighty Viking wore on his chest. A sixth-century Scandinavian goldsmith hammered the medallion to a four-inch diameter, then embossed and beaded it to imitate a Roman coin—which the Vikings vested with magical powers. The faces above the emperor's bust may be emblems of good fortune. The pendant hung from a gold necklace.

OVERLEAF: Tiny human heads and strange beasts, soldered to the three-ringed collar above, gave supernatural powers to the unknown Viking king who wore it—or so he would have believed. A Swedish goldsmith made the solid gold collar, which is eight inches in diameter, striating each of the three bands with filigree detail. The royal wearer buried the collar to hide it from marauding tribes—no doubt intending eventually to retrieve the treasure.

*The two brooches above, which a Jutlandian goldsmith made early in
the tenth century for a wealthy patron, are covered with tendrils of
gold filigree. Viking women fastened their woolen dresses with such
brooches, one on each shoulder; men secured their tunics with much
simpler jewelry. The golden domes conceal pins.*

A Gotlandian woman of means pinned her shawl at the breast with the drum-shaped brooch above. The magnificent work in gold and silver is actually a thin veneer affixed to a bronze core two inches across.

Animals, birds, and vegetation proliferate on the jewel box above, ten inches long. The metal is gilt bronze, the panels walrus-tusk ivory. Made about A.D. 1000 the box may have belonged to the daughter of Knud, king of England, Denmark, and Norway.

OVERLEAF: *The Viking who buried this hoard at Hon, Norway, in about 860 had looted or traded far and wide. Weighing over five pounds, the gold includes Viking necklaces, a brooch from France, and rings and coins of Greece and Arabia.*

THE BARBARIANS: A CHRONOLOGY

	SCYTHIANS AND SARMATIANS	CELTS	GERMANIC TRIBES AND THE HUNS	VIKINGS
B.C.	c. 700 Scythians migrate to south Russia from Siberia	c. 700 Austrian Celts bury iron swords with their dead		
	c. 680 Scythians join forces with Assyria for raids to the south			
	c. 650 Scythians plunder Palestine, and attempt to invade Egypt			
	612 Medes and Scythians join to attack Assyrian capital at Nineveh	c. 600 Celts in central Europe		
	c. 600 Medes drive Scythians out of western Asia, back to Russian steppe			
	514 Scythians defy Persia's Darius the Great in south Russia			
	c. 500 Scythians fashion treasures from gold	c. 450 Celts enter Spain		
	c. 450 Trade with the Greeks flourishes / Herodotus visits south Russia / Objects in Scythian graves show increasing Greek influence	c. 400 Celts migrate to British Isles / Celts from Gaul enter Italy		
		c. 390 Celts sack Rome		
		c. 280 Celtic tribes invade Greece		
		c. 275 Galatia established by Celts in northern Turkey		
		c. 260 Celts encounter Scythians in northern Black Sea region—acquire habit of wearing trousers, torques		
		c. 250 Shrine built at Roquepertuse, France		
		58–51 Julius Caesar fights Celts of Gaul		
		52 Caesar conquers Vercingetorix		
		c. 50 Gundestrup caldron buried		
		46 Vercingetorix executed		
A.D.	c. 50 Strabo observes and writes about the Sarmatians	c. 50 Strabo observes and writes about the Celts		
		61 Queen Boadicea leads British Celts against Rome		
			c. 100 Tacitus writes about Germans on the Roman frontier	
	c. 150 Scythians succumb to the Sarmatians		c. 170 Marcus Aurelius wages war against Germanic invaders, pushing them back to the Danube	
	c. 200 Sarmatians begin to move off the steppe; use heavy armor for cavalry	c. 200 Irish Celts move into Wales		
			c. 250 Salian Franks move into Belgium and then Gaul, from the lower Rhine region	
			c. 275 Visigoths from southern Sweden settle in Carpathian Mountains	
	c. 350 Sarmatians settle in eastern Europe		c. 375 Goths move west from the Baltic Sea region	
			c. 380 Huns come out of central Asia	
			395 Roman Empire split	
			c. 400 Vandals cross Germany into Roman Gaul / Angles and Saxons settle on the coast of Gaul	

410 Romans leave Britain

c. 450 Scotti move into northern Britain

c. 500 Celts, possibly under King Arthur, resist the Angles and the Saxons

c. 700 Ardagh Chalice made

402 Stilicho defends Italy against the Visigoths

410 Alaric attacks Rome with the Visigoths

c. 420 Vandals sweep through Gaul, Spain, and North Africa

441 Attila the Hun attacks eastern Roman Empire

446 Salian Franks take Turnacum (now Tournai, in Belgium)

c. 450 Angles and Saxons invade Britain from northern Germany and Jutland Huns attack Gaul

c. 455 Vandals enter Rome

457 Attila confronts Pope Leo the Great at Mantua and withdraws from Italy

481 Death of Childeric I, king of the Salian Franks
Clovis becomes king of the Salian Franks

482 Childeric buried at Tournai

488 Theodoric, king of the Ostrogoths, invades Italy

496 Clovis and his men baptized at Reims

533 Vandals conquered by Romans

558 Chlothar I, king of the Franks

c. 570 Leovigild, Visigothic king, constantly at war to protect Spain

c. 600 Angles and Saxons hold most of England

620 Sutton Hoo boat burial

627 Death of Raedwald, king of East Anglia

c. 654 King Recceswinth

757 Offa, king of Mercia

855 Edmund, king of England

978 Aethelred, king of England

787 Norwegian Vikings attack Lindisfarne

c. 800 Vikings reach Faroe Islands

c. 850 Vikings descend on Russia from Sweden Oseberg boat burial in Norway

860 Harald Fairhair becomes king of Norway

890 Rollo invades northeastern France

c. 900 Vikings established in Iceland Gokstad boat burial in Norway

c. 960 King Harald Bluetooth of Denmark converts to Christianity

986 Eric the Red leads colonists to Greenland

994 Olaf Tryggvesson becomes king of Norway

1000 Leif Ericson launches expedition to Vinland

1035 Death of Knud, ruler of England, Denmark, and Norway

1066 Normans invade England

ACKNOWLEDGMENTS & CREDITS

We would like to thank the following for their assistance: Johanna Awdry, British Museum Publications; Geoffrey Cooper, Photographic Services, British Museum; Canon Ronald L. Coppin, Durham Cathedral, Durham; C.M. Dixon, Dover; Katherine East, Department of Medieval and Later Antiquities, British Museum; Marna Feldt, Swedish Consulate Service, N.Y.; Ray Gardner, Department of Coins and Medals, British Museum; Barbara Heller, Werner Forman Archive, London; Michael Holford, Essex; F.M. Holt, Ashmolean Museum, Oxford; Angelo Hornak, London; Annette M. Kennett, Chester City Record Office, Chester; Krister Malmstrom and Finn Martner of the ATA, Statens Historiska Museer, Stockholm; Margaret McGahan, Bord Failte, Dublin; G.J. Owen, Cambridge University Museum of Archaeology and Anthropology, Cambridge; Terje Bakke Pettersen of Mittet Foto A.S., Oslo; Iris Philips, Department of Prehistoric and Romano-British Antiquities, British Museum; Dr. Richard H. Randall, Director and Jennie P. Baumann, Photographic Services, Walters Art Gallery, Baltimore; John Rhodes, City Museum and Art Gallery, Gloucester; Irene Shaw, The Museum of London, London; and Alan Stahl, Associate Curator of Medieval Coins, American Numismatic Society, N.Y.

Map by H. Shaw Borst
Endsheet design by Cockerell Bindery/TALAS
Mechanical production by Barbara Kraus

Cover: British Museum, London. 2: Werner Forman Archive. 4–5: Sabine Weiss/Rapho. 6: Walters Art Gallery, Baltimore. 10–11: Lee Boltin, Croton-on-Hudson, N.Y. 12: Werner Forman Archive. 13–16: Editions Cercle d'Art, Paris. 17: Lee Boltin, Croton-on-Hudson, N.Y. 18: Editions Cercle d'Art, Paris. 19–20: Lee Boltin, Croton-on-Hudson, N.Y. 21: Sabine Weiss/Rapho. 22: Sovfoto. 23: Tass. 24–27: Lee Boltin, Croton-on-Hudson, N.Y. 28–29: Ingrid Geske/Staatliche Museen Preussischer Kulturbesitz, Berlin (West). 30–37: Lee Boltin, Croton-on-Hudson, N.Y. 38-39: Editions Cercle d'Art, Paris. 40: EPA/Scala. 42–43: Staatliche Museen, Berlin (East). 44: Musée Borely, Marseilles/Belzeaux-Rapho. 44–45: Musée Borely, Marseilles/Lauros-Giraudon. 46–47: Wolfgang Fritz, Cologne. 48–49: Louis Goldman/Photo Researchers. 50–51: Farrell Grehan/Photo Researchers. 52–53: Louis-Michel Jugie/Musée Historique et Archeologique de l'Orléanais, Orléans. 54–61: Erich Lessing/Magnum. 62, left: Giraudon. 62, right–63: British Museum, London. 64: Erich Lessing/Magnum. 65: British Museum, London. 66–73: Erich Lessing/Magnum. 74–75: British Museum, London. 76–77: Lee Boltin, Croton-on-Hudson, N.Y. 78–79: Pierre Belzeaux/Zodiaque. 80–81: Claus Hansmann, Stockdorf. 82–83: Oronoz. 84: Brogi/Mansell Collection. 85: Oscar Savio/Museo Nazionale Romano, Rome. 86–87: Anderson/EPA. 88: Alinari/Scala. 89: British Museum, London. 90–91: British Library, London. 92: Mas. 93: Dumbarton Oaks, Washington, D.C. 94–95: Walters Art Gallery, Baltimore. 96–97: Römisch-Germanisches Museum, Cologne. 98–99, left to right: Oriol Maspons/Ediciones Polígrafa, Barcelona; Mas; Oriol Maspons/Ediciones Polígrafa, Barcelona. 100: Prähistorische Sammlung, Munich. 101: Metropolitan Museum of Art, N.Y. 102–103: Walters Art Gallery, Baltimore. 104: Mas. 105–107: Hirmer Fotoarchiv. 108–109: Pierre Belzeaux/Rapho. 110: Ray Gardner/British Museum, London. 111: B.J. Wilson/Ronald Sheridan's Photo Library. 112–113: Bibliothèque Nationale, Paris/Lauros-Giraudon. 114–115: Treasury of St. Denis, Paris/Ziolo. 116–117: British Museum, London. 118: Pierpont Morgan Library, N.Y. 119: British Museum, London. 120: Michael Holford, Essex. 121–133: British Museum, London. 134–135: C.M. Dixon/Photoresources. 136: Michael Holford, Essex. 137: Werner Forman Archive. 138–139: Michael Holford, Essex. 140–141, left: Werner Forman Archive. 141, top: C.M. Dixon/Photoresources. 141, bottom: Jacques Brun/Mittet Foto. 142–143: Universitetets Oldsaksamling, Oslo. 144–145: Ove Holst/Universitetets Oldsaksamling, Oslo. 146–147: Stofnun Arna Magnússonar/The Manuscript Institute, Reykjavik. 148: Lennart Larsen/Nationalmuseet, Copenhagen. 149: Jacques Brun/Mittet Foto. 150–153, left: British Museum Publications, London. 153, right: Michael Holford, Essex. 154: C.M. Dixon/Photoresources. 155: Lennart Larsen/Nationalmuseet, Copenhagen. 156–157: Nationalmuseet, Copenhagen. 158, top: Werner Forman Archive. 158–159: AB Nordbok, Gothenburg. 159, top: Werner Forman Archive. 160: Mauro Pucciarelli, Rome. 161: Antikvarisk-topografiska archivet/Statens Historiska Museer, Stockholm. 162–163: Henry Groskinski, N.Y. 164: Werner Forman Archive. 165: Antikvarisk-topografiska archivet/Statens Historiska Museer, Stockholm. 166–167: Bayerisches Nationalmuseum, Munich. 168–169: Universitetets Oldsaksamling, Oslo.

SUGGESTED READINGS

Artamonov, M.I., *The Splendor of Scythian Art.* Frederick A. Praeger, Inc., 1969.

Bruce-Mitford, Rupert, *The Sutton Hoo Ship Burial.* British Museum Publications Ltd., 1972.

Chadwick, Nora, *The Celts.* Penguin Books, Inc., 1970.

Cunliffe, Barry, *The Celtic World.* McGraw-Hill Book Co., 1979.

Dixon, Philip, *Barbarian Europe.* Phaidon Press Ltd., 1976.

From the Land of the Scythians. The Metropolitan Museum of Art Bulletin, Vol. XXXII, No. 5, 1975.

Graham-Campbell, James, *The Viking World.* Ticknor & Fields, 1980.

Lasko, Peter, *The Kingdom of the Franks.* McGraw-Hill Book Co., 1971.

Lopez, Robert, *The Birth of Europe.* M. Evans and Co., Inc., 1962.

Malraux, André and André Parrot, eds., *Europe of the Invasions.* George Braziller, Inc., 1969.

Rice, David Talbot, ed., *The Dawn of European Civilization.* McGraw-Hill Book Co., 1965.

Ross, Marvin Chauncey, *Arts of the Migration Period.* The Walters Art Gallery, 1961.

Wilson, David M., *The Northern World.* Harry N. Abrams, Inc., 1980.

INDEX

Page numbers in **boldface type** refer to illustrations and captions.

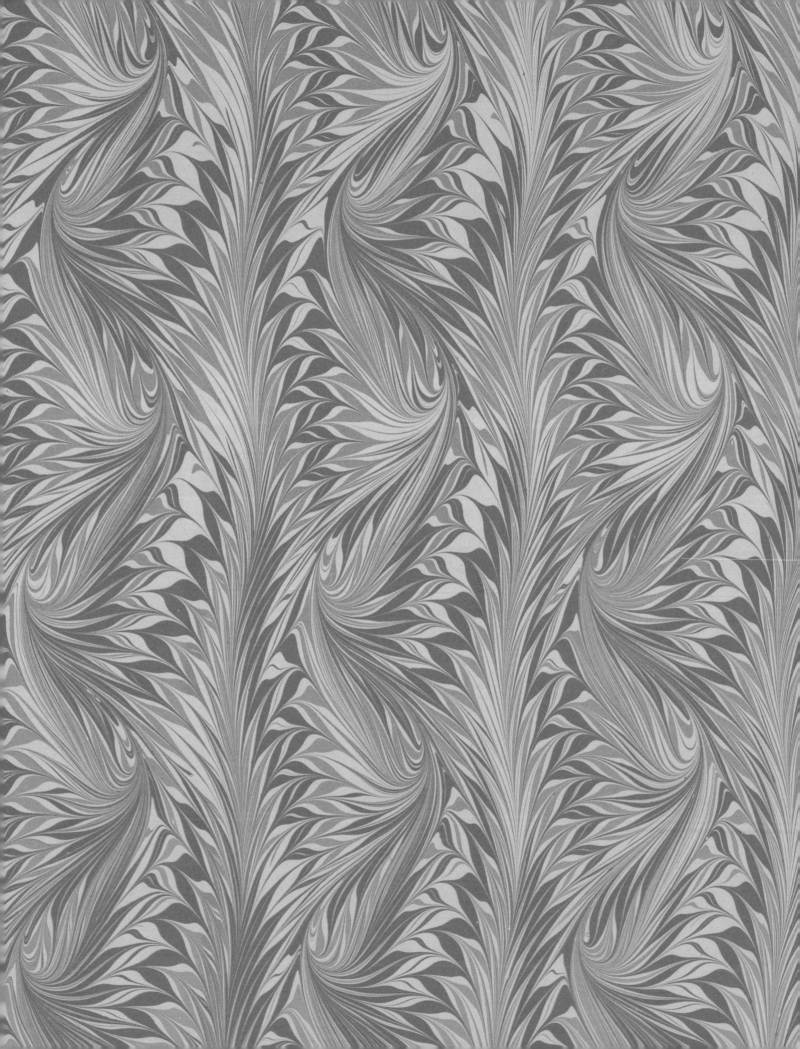